$ELL, $ELL, $ELL!

$ELL, $ELL, $ELL!

Valuable Tips and Lessons Learned from a Successful Lifetime in Sales

DAVID F. D'ORAZI

Published by D&D Unlimited

ISBN (print): 979-8-218-77751-7
ISBN (ebook): 979-8-218-77752-4

Book design and production by www.AuthorSuccess.com

I'm dedicating this book to my dear friend and colleague, Doug Teate—one of the greatest salesmen I've ever had the privilege of knowing, and one of the best buddies I've ever had.

For the nearly sixteen years we spent working together, ending each sales day the same way—talking strategy, exchanging ideas, and pushing each other to be better. But what made those conversations unforgettable wasn't just the sales wisdom we shared; it was the laughter in between. Doug had a way of making even the toughest days lighter, and his passion for selling was unmatched.

Though a decade has passed since he left us, his influence remains as strong in my life as ever. This book is a tribute to him—to his brilliance, humor, and unwavering dedication to the art of selling. I miss those late-night talks, my friend. This one's for you.

CONTENTS

FOREWORD
BY VINCE D'ORAZI

As the oldest of the author's four sons, I've had a front-row seat to his sales journey. I've watched from the sidelines and occasionally stepped in to help, but let me tell you: this man lives and breathes sales.

For years, he talked about writing this book, about capturing the lessons, stories, and hard-earned wisdom from a career that has been anything but ordinary. Now, he's finally done it. And the truth is, even after decades in the game, his passion for the art of selling still burns as brightly as ever.

Yes, technology is changing our world at lightning speed, but helping him shape and edit this book reminded me of something important: the fundamentals of human connection, persuasion, and influence are timeless. Even if you're not in sales, the strategies shared here, which are all rooted in real-life experience, are tools you can use every day. Whether you're negotiating a raise, getting your kids to eat their vegetables, or persuading your spouse about where to take the next family vacation, you're selling. We all are.

The bottom line is this: if you live in the modern world, you're in sales—whether you realize it or not. And this book is packed with insights that will help you become more effective, more confident, and more successful in that role. For those in the sales profession, what you're about to read is pure gold. For everyone else, it's a masterclass in the art of influence.

A Book Changed My Life—And I Hope That This One Will Change Yours

The first motivational book I ever read—and still my favorite to this day—is *The Greatest Salesman in the World* by Og Mandino. I stumbled upon it in a small, used bookstore in Hawaii back in the 1980s, and that one book single-handedly transformed my sales career.

Now, nearly seventy years after making my first sale as a child, I'm pouring the most important lessons I've learned into this book you're about to read. Not only will this book include a collection of tips and strategies, but it will also explain how I learned them all through my real-world experiences. Ultimately, I hope you'll be able to utilize some of these tools to help build a life of success and financial freedom through sales.

If you take the lessons in this book to heart, I have no doubt that you'll rise to the top. But beyond that? You'll learn how to communicate, how to influence, and how to create opportunities—skills that will serve you in every area of life.

I hope this book not only helps you sell more and earn more, but also gives you the confidence, knowledge, and mindset to win in your personal life as well.

It took me over forty years to put all my sales secrets into writing, but I can tell you this: these strategies work. I remember being thirty-five years old when one of my bosses took me to lunch. Sitting across from me, he asked, "Dave, how do you manage to be in the top 2 percent of this company's salesforce year after year?"

At the time, my answer was simple: "I just do it."

I didn't overthink it—I just loved selling. I loved people. It was my passion. But here's the thing—I didn't even enter corporate sales until I was a little over thirty years old. However, the jobs and life experiences I had before that shaped me into the successful salesperson I would eventually become. The mindset, the work ethic, the hustle—it all led to a forty-year-plus career of consistently winning in sales . . . and I'm still going strong!

Now, in my seventies, I'm generating nearly three times more income than ever before—and I'm still having fun. My passion today isn't just selling—it's helping other salespeople improve and reach their full potential.

If you commit to creating your own success stories every day and stay dedicated to the craft, I can confidently say that you will succeed.

Technology may evolve, industries may shift, but the core principles of sales remain the same. If you apply these lessons, you won't just build a financially rewarding career—you'll create a life of freedom, opportunity, and success.

I'll begin with some breakdowns of valuable strategies and skills I've learned over my career, and from there, I'll take you through my evolution as a salesperson, as I recount memorable anecdotes spanning from my childhood in the 1950s to present-day stories of successfully selling in the twenty-first century. So, let's get to it!

CHAPTER 1

The Greatest Job in the World

If you're reading this, I don't think I need to sell you on why working in sales is such a great career path. However, if you haven't reached this realization yet, let me break it down for you. Sales isn't just a job; it's a ticket to financial freedom, independence, and an incredible lifestyle. Here's why:

1. Unlimited Earning Potential: There's no cap on how much you can make in sales. You control your income based on how hard you work and how well you sell. Want to make six figures? Seven? It's all up to you. Unlike a traditional nine-to-five job, your paycheck isn't limited to an annual salary.

2. You Control Your Own Destiny: Forget waiting around for a promotion or hoping your boss notices your hard work. In sales, you have complete control over your future. Your performance dictates your success. The better you sell, the faster you climb the ladder—or better yet, you can then even build your own business.

3. Sales Is Recession-Proof: No matter how the economy is doing, companies will always need great salespeople. When times are tough, businesses don't cut their best revenue generators. If you can sell, you will always have a job.

4. No Age Limit, No Discrimination: In sales, results speak louder than anything else. No one cares how old you are or where you come from—as long as you can close deals and drive revenue, you will always be valuable.

5. You Can Be Your Own Boss: Even if you work for a company, great salespeople operate like entrepreneurs. You build your own book of business, create your own schedule, and decide how you want to sell. If you keep closing deals, you call the shots.

6. You Can Build Real Wealth: Sales doesn't just give you a high income—it gives you the ability to invest and grow your money. At one point in my career, I owned over a dozen properties—all because I used my sales income to invest smartly. If you play your cards right, sales can set you up for an early and comfortable retirement.

CHAPTER 2

The Power of Relationship Selling

As you likely know, the types of sales one can make typically fall into two broad categories: transactional and relationship (also known as "relational"). Transactional selling is all about speed and efficiency—quick, one-time deals with minimal interaction beyond the sale. Relationship selling, in contrast, focuses on cultivating long-term partnerships through trust, follow-up, and personalized service.

Throughout my career, I've worked in both worlds. What I've discovered is that these two approaches aren't as different as they seem, since they both share a common goal of trying to match a solution with a customer's need.

Many of the core skills—such as listening, asking the right questions, and understanding the buyer's mindset—are transferable across both styles. The best salespeople know how to shift gears when needed, blending the strengths of each approach to match the situation and the customer.

WHY WINNING HEARTS WINS BUSINESS

There's selling, and then there's *relationship* selling. If you've ever closed a deal because someone said, "I trust you," then you already understand the difference.

Relationship selling is all about playing the long game. It's not about pushing products. It's about building *partnerships*.

Where transactional selling focuses on features, price, and a quick close, relationship selling is about trust, empathy, and genuinely understanding the customer's world. It's about showing up not just as a vendor, but as an advisor, a supporter, and a friend.

WHAT SETS RELATIONSHIP SELLING APART

- **It's Customer-First, Not Commission-First:** You dig deep to understand their goals, pain points (or problem areas where they could use some help), and what keeps them up at night—because you actually care.
- **It's Built on Trust and Rapport:** You're not just listening to reply. You're listening to *understand*. You become someone they count on.
- **It's About the Long-Term Win:** Relationship sellers don't just want one deal—they want to become part of the customer's ongoing success story.

WHY IT WORKS: THE REAL-WORLD PAYOFF

- **Loyal Customers Stick Around:** When someone feels seen, heard, and understood, they won't jump ship for a small discount elsewhere.

- **It Opens More Doors:** Strong relationships lead to referrals, repeat business, and conversations that go far beyond the original pitch.
- **It Creates a Better Customer Experience:** Because when you treat someone like a person, not a quota, you stand out in a sea of pushy salespeople.
- **It Sparks Word-of-Mouth Magic:** People talk about great experiences. When they do, *you* become the name they recommend.

RELATIONSHIP SELLING IN ACTION: BEST PRACTICES THAT MATTER

- **Do Your Homework:** Learn about the client's industry, their role, and their pain points before the first meeting. Show them they matter enough to take the time to prepare.
- **Master Active Listening:** Don't assume. Ask questions. Clarify. Pause before you speak. The goal is to *get it*, not just *get through it.*
- **Offer Value Beyond the Deal:** Share insights. Pass along helpful articles. Introduce them to someone in your network. Be valuable even when you're not selling.
- **Follow Up—Consistently:** After the sale, check in. Ask how things are going. Show that your care doesn't stop when the contract is signed.
- **Be Real:** People can smell phony from a mile away. Be authentic. Be human. Be someone *they want to work with.*

The bottom line is that relationship selling isn't just about being friendly. It's about being intentional. It's about building bridges that last beyond the first sale.

The best salespeople I've ever known weren't just closers. They were connectors. They established genuine trust, which translated into lasting, long-term value.

If you want repeat customers, real referrals, and a career that lasts decades, master this approach that I'll expand upon throughout this book. People buy from those they trust.

CHAPTER 3

The Rewards That Await You

THE FAST TRACK TO FINANCIAL FREEDOM

I've been making over $100,000 a year since the mid-1980s, and it didn't take long to break into the $200,000 and $300,000 commission brackets. How? By mastering the art of sales, leveraging the right strategies, and staying relentless in my pursuit of success. If you do the same, the rewards can be life-changing.

I've earned over ten all-expenses-paid trips to Hawaii with my spouse, all from sales performance. That's not luck. That's the power of being a top performer. If you put in the work, the rewards will follow.

WHAT IT HAS MEANT FOR ME

When you're at the top of your game, you get to enjoy a lifestyle most people only dream of. Here are just a few perks I've been able to earn thanks to a career in sales:

- **Dining with Clients and Prospects:** Breakfast, lunch, and dinner meetings don't feel like work when you're building relationships.
- **A New Car Every Two Years:** With insurance covered by my company.
- **Leisure Activities:** For me, it's golfing twice a month—Because why not? Flexibility is a perk when you control your schedule.
- **Buying What You Want:** Not just what you need. A career in sales gives you financial freedom.
- **Season Tickets for Forty-Plus Years:** I've been a Los Angeles Dodger season ticket holder for decades, all thanks to my commissions.
- **Luxury Vacations:** I've won sales contests that sent me to Mexico, Hawaii, Las Vegas, and other incredible destinations.
- **Respect and Recognition:** When you're a top salesperson, your peers and leaders admire and respect you, and the awards and accolades will follow.

WHAT DOES IT MEAN FOR YOU?

Sales isn't just a job; it's a path to financial freedom. Imagine finally buying your dream home or finally taking that dream vacation without a second thought. These aren't luxuries reserved for the ultra-rich—they're within your reach when you commit to excelling in sales.

And it doesn't stop there. When you're making serious money, you're not just spending—you're investing. Whether it's real estate, stocks, or starting your own business, the fruits of your labor will provide you with the extra capital to build long-term wealth.

So, the question is: Are you ready to put in the work and claim your place at the top?

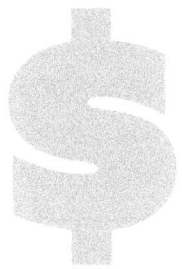

CHAPTER 4

The Fifteen Qualities of a Highly Successful Salesperson

After decades in sales, I've identified the fifteen most essential qualities that separate top performers from the rest. These aren't just theories—they're battle-tested traits that have fueled my success and the success of the best salespeople I've ever met. Master these, and you'll be on your way to sales greatness.

1. ACTIVE LISTENING

Great salespeople don't just talk—they listen. The more you listen, the more you learn about your prospect's pain points, needs, and desires. Listen twice as much as you speak, and you'll close more deals.

> **An Example of How I Learned This:** Early in my career, I was handed a technical account—something I'd never managed before. The company wasn't sure I could handle it. I said, "Bring it on."
>
> On our first call, I didn't pitch—I just listened. I noticed something quickly: this technical expert

didn't want to talk shop. He wanted a human connection—someone who could give him a break from his highly analytical world. So, I took him to lunch. No products, no charts—just two guys talking. That small gesture built trust. By the end of the year, I had tripled the account's sales. He didn't need another salesperson; he needed a friend who listened.

2. POSITIVE ATTITUDE

Have you ever seen a top-performing salesperson with a bad attitude? Me neither. Energy is contagious. A positive attitude attracts customers, builds relationships, and keeps you motivated when times get tough.

> **An Example of How I Learned This:** One time, when a product I was selling didn't work the first time, I didn't panic—I smiled and said, "The next one will."

> I followed up. I treated each failure like the beginning of a new opportunity. Most importantly, I made sure the alternative product worked. That relentless optimism turned failures into wins more times than I can count. In sales, confidence in your process is contagious.

3. ADAPTABILITY

Sales are unpredictable. A great salesperson can read the room, adjust their approach, and pivot strategies when needed. Whether it's a new objection or an unexpected twist, the best salespeople stay flexible.

An Example of How I Learned This: At one point, one of my sales accounts went through three management changes in six months, right during contract renewals. Each time, I built a new relationship from scratch. The final manager was someone I'd known for years, who'd started at the company in a lower-level position. Because I had stayed in touch as he climbed the ladder, when it was finally his call, I had the edge and renewed the contract. Adaptability isn't just reacting—it's preparing for change before it hits.

4. CONFIDENCE

If you don't believe in yourself and your product, why should your customer? Confidence sells. Speak with conviction, make strong recommendations, and never hesitate to ask for the sale.

An Example of How I Learned This: Once, I introduced a product to a client that I believed in so much that my energy pulled others in. So much so that it became my company's number one seller. People don't just buy the product—they buy your belief in it. Confidence isn't arrogance; it's conviction backed by preparation.

5. PATIENCE

Some deals take time. Rushing a sale can erode trust and deter prospects. Patience and persistence go hand in hand—keep following up, nurturing the relationship, and guiding the customer to a decision.

An Example of How I Learned This: I once called on a major company every two weeks for four months. Every time I visited, I brought them fresh info. The buyer kept saying, "I'm good with my vendor."

But then, on visit number eight, he chuckled and said, "You're here more than my current guy."

Then he gave me a shot. That "no" turned into a great account. In sales, patience pays—but only if you bring persistence with it.

6. EMOTIONAL INTELLIGENCE

Understanding people is just as crucial as understanding products. Sales is about building relationships and knowing how to read emotions. Empathizing and responding appropriately can be a game-changer.

An Example of How I Learned This: On one occasion, I was engaged in a conversation with a prospect, but progress stalled. Something felt off. Then it hit me—he wasn't the decision-maker. Instead of pushing harder, I pivoted. I respectfully contacted his boss, set up a quick meeting, delivered the pitch, and closed the deal. Sales isn't just about knowing your product—it's about reading the room and sensing when it's time to adjust your approach.

7. PROBLEM-SOLVING SKILLS

Customers buy solutions, not products. The best salespeople identify the problems their customers didn't even realize they had, then position their product as the perfect answer. Be the problem solver, and you'll be the deal closer.

> **An Example of How I Learned This:** One prospect I called on while working for a water treatment company was out of environmental compliance for their wastewater, which was flowing into the ocean. For nearly a year, I worked with labs, testing different chemistries, and ultimately found a solution that allowed for safe discharge—one that didn't harm aquatic life. That solution turned into a $1 million account with $800,000 in profit. Big wins often come from big problems—if you're the one who solves them.

8. INTEGRITY

Reputation is everything. Top sales professionals keep their promises, are honest about what their product can (and cannot) do, and prioritize their customers' needs. Trust leads to repeat business and referrals, while cutting corners leads to dead-end careers.

> **An Example of How I Learned This:** In my early days of selling, I answered a question with incorrect information, and that one mistake cost me the account. Lesson learned: if you don't know the answer, admit it—then go find it fast. That account could've been huge. But I'm glad I learned early that in sales, credibility takes years to build and seconds to lose.

9. RESILIENCE

Sales is full of rejection. But top salespeople don't get discouraged—they bounce back stronger. Every "no" is one step closer to a "yes."

An Example of How I Learned This: A prospect once told me flat-out no—and I found out why. They were using a product my company didn't carry. I couldn't compete with that. A month later, they called and needed a different product that I *did* sell. That became one of my best accounts. You never know when a "no" is just a "not yet."

10. PRODUCT KNOWLEDGE

You can't sell what you don't understand. The best salespeople know their product inside and out—its strengths, weaknesses, and exactly how it solves customer problems. Knowledge equals confidence, and confidence equals sales.

An Example of How I Learned This: While I was succeeding at selling one product for a company I worked for, I noticed some other top sales reps excelling in selling products in areas that I had no knowledge of. I knew I needed to evolve, so I enrolled in night school, learned about those topics in depth, and soon had one of the largest accounts in the country for that company. Knowledge isn't just power—it's a ladder to the top.

11. CONTINUOUS LEARNING

Markets change. Customer needs evolve. Top sales professionals never stop learning. They read, attend training sessions, and continually seek ways to enhance their craft.

An Example of How I Learned This: Back when computers first hit the scene, I struggled. My peers laughed—I didn't care. I learned what I needed, out-sourced what I couldn't do, and kept moving forward. You don't have to be a tech genius, but you do have to be humble enough to keep learning.

12. ORGANIZATION

Keeping track of leads, follow-ups, customer details, and schedules is critical. The best salespeople use customer relationship management (CRM) tools, set reminders, and stay on top of their game so no opportunity slips through the cracks.

> **An Example of How I Learned This:** Sales is a game of focus. I watched reps list accounts they *wished* they had on their boards. Not me. I was honest with myself. I tracked the real prospects, prioritized them, and followed up relentlessly. I saved every number in my phone so I'd never miss a hot lead. Organization doesn't just make you efficient—it makes you money.

13. HARD WORK

There's no shortcut to success. Sales requires effort, persistence, and dedication. The best in the business are willing to put in the work, whether it's extra calls, networking, or refining their pitch.

> **An Example of How I Learned This:** I've spent countless nights crafting proposals. Not every account was worth it, but the right ones were. I learned to qualify prospects better. I didn't just chase any lead but pursued the ones that paid well and valued what I brought to the table. Sales is a grind. But if you work smart *and* hard, it pays off in commissions—and pride.

14. SELF-MOTIVATION

No one is going to push you harder than yourself. Top salespeople set goals, stay driven, and take action every single day—even when they don't feel like it.

> **An Example of How I Learned This:** For decades, I've set my alarm for 5:00 or 6:00 a.m. I do my workout, eat breakfast, and by 8:00 a.m., I'm ready to sell. One of my college sales instructors said, "If you eat breakfast after 8:00 a.m., you've already lost the day."
>
> I never forgot that. Money motivated me, but recognition kept me going. There's nothing like being named a top rep. In sales, no one's going to push you—you have to be your own engine.

15. SOCIAL SKILLS

Sales is all about relationships. The ability to connect, build rapport, and communicate effectively separates great salespeople from the rest. People buy from people they like and trust.

> **An Example of How I Learned This:** In sales, some of your biggest wins won't come from cold calls or scheduled appointments—they'll come from conversations you didn't even know would matter. That's why I've always made it a point to join every industry-related organization I could find for the products I was selling. Trade groups, local networking events, lunch-and-learns—you name it, I showed up. Not to sell, but to connect.

At one event, I struck up a casual conversation with a guy standing by the coffee. I asked what he did, and it turned out he couldn't use any of my products. We chatted for five minutes, swapped cards, and that was it. A few weeks later, he called me, not for his company, but for a *referral*. A friend of his at another major company *could* utilize my products, and that referral ultimately led to a massive account.

The lesson? Never underestimate a casual chat. Everyone you meet knows someone you don't—and if you're genuinely curious, personable, and professional, doors open. In sales, the world doesn't just get smaller—it gets more connected.

CHAPTER 5

Creating Sales Success

SETTING THE TABLE FOR SUCCESS

Winning in sales isn't about random outreach—it's about intentional, strategic interaction. When trying to find clients, conduct research and build yourself a target list of no more than twenty-five top prospects, with a top ten that gets your most focused effort. Every touchpoint should bring real value to your prospect, whether it's technical information, industry insights, or just showing up at the right moments (like on holidays, when others forget). If you're not staying in front of them, your competitor will.

GET TO THE DECISION-MAKER

Once you've identified your prospects, there's another crucial step: getting to the right person—the decision-maker. This is the individual who holds the authority to sign agreements, approve budgets, or advance deals. Your job? Find them and find them fast.

Don't waste time spinning your wheels with people who can't say "yes." Ask smart questions. Pay attention. Navigate through the organization you're approaching and uncover who truly calls the shots. Don't wear blinders, and keep an open mind, because sometimes the key decision-maker isn't who you expected.

THE POWER OF "WHAT'S IN IT FOR ME?"

Once you've identified the right person, shift your focus to what drives them. Why should they change what they're doing and buy your product? What problems are they facing that they might not even realize? People may seem content, but there's always *something* that could be better. Your job is to find that gap, to ask the right questions, and listen intently.

Here's my golden rule: listen twice as much as you talk. It's not just a great sales strategy—it's a great life strategy. Whether it's in business, relationships, or negotiations, people want to feel heard. If you ask a prospect, "How was your day?" and they say, "Fine," that tells you nothing.

It's best to avoid closed-ended questions like this and instead ask, "What's been the best part of your day?" or "What challenges have you run into today?"

This gets them talking—and that's where the gold lies.

LOOK FOR THE OPENING—THEN RUN FOR THE SCORE

Think of sales like football. You're scanning the field, looking for that open lane—the daylight. When you see it, you go for it. The same applies to conversations with prospects. Keep them engaged, uncover their pain points, and when the opportunity presents itself, drive the sale home.

SUCCESS IS A MARATHON, NOT A SPRINT

Most salespeople make one call to a new prospect, and then they give up. If there's zero competition, you might be able to get away with it. But in reality? One-and-done rarely works. Consider this: 95 percent of salespeople never follow up beyond the initial call. Of the remaining 5 percent, only a small fraction makes it past the third attempt. But here's the kicker—the real wins typically happen after the fifth call. The top sales professionals understand that persistence, value, and consistency separate the great ones from the average ones.

SALES IS LIKE A GARDEN—WATER IT OR WATCH IT DIE

Think of your sales pipeline as a garden and treat it accordingly. If you stop watering it, it will wither away. Every interaction with your clients is an opportunity to nurture the relationship by bringing a proposal, a solution, or something useful that keeps the conversation moving forward.

The bottom line? One call won't cut it. The more you show up, provide value, and stay persistent, the more likely you are to close—and keep—your customers for the long haul.

LEVERAGE YOUR TEAM—SUCCESS ISN'T A SOLO SPORT

Great salespeople know that selling isn't a one-person game. When you have access to corporate resources, use them! Also, you can create or become part of a mastermind sales group, which is a gathering of like-minded people in sales who meet frequently in small groups to support, encourage, and learn from each other's stories of success and failure. The best sales pros aren't afraid to ask for help. In fact, reaching out to peers isn't just good for you—it boosts their confidence, too. People love to be recognized for their expertise, and when you ask for guidance, you're showing respect for their knowledge and experience.

ALWAYS BRING VALUE—NO POINTLESS CALLS

Every sales visit should have a purpose. Don't just check in—bring something of real value to your prospects and customers. A great way to do this? Offer to do case studies or regularly provide them with updates on the latest technology, trends, or solutions that could impact their business.

Most prospects or clients don't have time for small talk. So, if you're popping in to say hello with no real reason, you're wasting their time—and yours. Instead, be the sales professional who always delivers something useful. That's how you stay at the forefront of their minds and build long-term relationships with them.

TRUST, EXPERTISE, AND THE POWER OF KNOWLEDGE

Zig Ziglar, one of the greatest salesmen and motivational speakers of all time, said it best: "If people like you, they'll listen to you. If they trust you, they'll do business with you."

Trust is everything in sales—whether it's with customers, your team, or your company. And the fastest way to build trust? Become an expert in what you sell. Know your product inside and out, and if you can, demonstrate how your product or program works better than their current one. The best salespeople aren't just good talkers—they're problem solvers. When you truly understand your product and how it helps your customers, you become their go-to expert.

CHAPTER 6

How To Keep Closing Deals:
My Five-Step Method

Every great salesperson has their own process and closing method that they refine over years of experience, trial, and error. Mine has consistently kept me growing my sales for over forty years.

If you master this, you'll have a repeatable, proven system to help you close more deals and maximize your earnings. This system worked for me, and I know it will work for you as well. Sales is about consistency, strategy, and execution. If you apply these principles and stick to the plan, you'll not only hit your goals, you'll exceed them.

STEP ONE: BUILD YOUR TARGET LIST
LIKE A SALES SNIPER

Success in sales starts with focus and determination. At the beginning of your process, create a realistic target list of up to twenty-five key accounts you want to close.

- **Your Top Ten Should Be Your Hot Prospects**

  These are the ones you should be working on every two weeks. If too much time passes, they'll forget about you, so stay on their radar.

- **Review Your List Every Quarter**

  If a prospect isn't moving forward, swap them out for a more promising one. Refine, replace, and reload.

- **Don't Waste Time on Hopeless Cases**

  If there's no chance of closing a deal, remove them. Focus on winnable opportunities.

This simple but powerful system has helped me close three to five major target accounts per year, keeping me at the top of my company's sales charts.

STEP TWO: THE "80/20 RULE" AND FOCUSING ON THE RIGHT CUSTOMERS

One of the most valuable lessons I've learned in sales is that 80 percent of your revenue will come from just 20 percent of your customers.

- **Identify Your Potential 20 Percent**

  These are your high-value, high-potential clients.

- **Nurture Them**

  Keep them engaged and keep adding value.

- **Never Take Them for Granted**

They are the backbone of your commission checks.

The best salespeople understand that their income isn't evenly distributed; they focus their energy where it matters most.

STEP THREE: ACCURACY IS EVERYTHING

A sales pipeline built on false hope is a one-way ticket to failure. Never put a prospect on your list just for the sake of it. Be brutally honest with yourself.

- If a company isn't a genuine potential buyer, don't waste your time.
- If a prospect is not engaging, not interested, or not a good fit, cut them loose.

Focus on quality over quantity, and work on deals that can realistically close.

STEP FOUR: THE ART OF CLOSING

Sales is an art form, just like painting. My father was a well-known artist, and I once asked him why he never signed his paintings right away. He told me: "It has to be complete in my mind first—only then will I sign it."

The same goes for closing a sale. You don't rush it. You refine, adjust, and make final touches—but once it's ready, you go all in and close the deal.

STEP FIVE: PLAN YOUR WORK, WORK YOUR PLAN

The most successful salespeople don't just wing it. They:

- **Set clear goals**
- **Have a structured process**
- **Execute their plan daily**

If you follow this method with discipline and focus, you'll find yourself in the top ranks of your sales force year after year. Wake up every morning excited to sell, plan your work, and work your plan. Enjoy the ride, sell with passion, and make a career out of winning!

CHAPTER 7

Goal Setting—Your Secret Weapon

If there's one thing that separates top salespeople from the rest, it's goal setting. I learned this early in my career, and it completely transformed my approach.

WHY SETTING GOALS WORKS

Years ago, after attending an event with the master of sales, Zig Ziglar, I started setting personal and business goals every January, based on his suggestion. At first, I wasn't sure if it would make a difference, but the results were unbelievable. Every year, I set about ten clear, measurable goals, and guess what? I've achieved at least eight out of ten, year after year. This isn't luck—it's the power of goal setting, and the efforts you take to make them happen.

THE POWER OF A SIMPLE SIGN

One of my earliest lessons in goal setting happened during my first year in corporate sales. At a company sales meeting, our regional manager challenged us to: "Put a sign on your desk that says: 'I will be number one in sales this year and achieve all of my goals.'"

I did exactly that. I put up the sign, saw it every day, and made it my mission. And that year, I finished as the number one salesperson in the company. This wasn't magic—it was focus, belief, and consistent action that drove me to achieve this goal.

SETTING YOUR GOALS

If you want to dominate in sales, you must set goals, and here are a few tips to get you started:

- **Set a clear target every year:** For both your personal and professional lives
- **Write it down:** Make it real.
- **Keep it visible:** Look at it daily.
- **Take action every day:** Even small steps add up.

So, what goals will you set for yourself this year? How will you push yourself to the top?

Make your goals. Take action, and I guarantee that if you commit to this process, you'll be at or near the top of your sales force year after year.

CHAPTER 8

The Birth of a Salesman [The 1950s]

Now that I've started off by sharing some of what I've learned throughout my sales career, I want to take you back through my evolution to share some of the countless lessons I've learned over the years, all of which have helped shape me into the successful salesperson I am today.

I've read countless books on "how to sell"—from Tony Robbins to Dennis Waitley, and Zig Ziglar to Wayne Dyer, and everyone in between. These experts offer incredible advice, but so many of them have never spent time in the trenches like I have. Zig Ziglar did, and his wisdom still stands the test of time, but my goal is to take things a step further. This isn't just about theories or ideas that sound good on paper; this is about real-world experience—strategies that have been tested, refined, and proven throughout my extensive career.

I didn't even enter professional sales until I was in my thirties. But every job I had before then taught me something valuable—how to connect, how to listen, and how to solve problems. And what better place to start my story than with my first memory of ever making a sale . . .

It didn't happen in a fancy office or a store with some slick pitch. No, my first sale happened when I was just eight years old. My best friend Greg's parents owned a funeral home, and one afternoon, while he and I were hanging out in his dad's office, we noticed some leftover flowers from a service earlier in the day that had been left behind. That's when inspiration struck.

"My mom adores flowers, and so do all the other ladies in the neighborhood," I told Greg. "We should sell these before they end up in the trash!"

And that's precisely what we did. We went door to door, selling bouquets for a dollar each, which was some good money to us back then! With the earnings we made that afternoon, we treated ourselves to some burgers and shakes at a local diner. It was our first taste of financial freedom, which we achieved by mixing some ingenuity with some 'boots on the ground' work.

But that fun didn't last long. The next day, Greg's dad found out what we'd done and shut us down immediately. According to him, selling leftover flowers from funerals was illegal. But that didn't leave me discouraged. Now that I'd experienced the thrill of making my own money, I wanted more.

The Lesson:
Entrepreneurs See Opportunity Everywhere

What I learned from this experience is that true salespeople don't wait for opportunities; they create them. That day, I realized that sales is about recognizing value where others don't. Always keep your eyes open for an opportunity, since you never know when something like a discarded bouquet might turn into a potential moneymaker.

SMILING: YOUR NUMBER ONE ASSET IN SALES

My father was a car salesman, and from an early age, I would watch him work his magic at the dealership. He had two powerful tools: a genuine smile and a stellar sense of humor. These weren't gimmicks; they were the foundation of his success.

I remember one night at the dinner table; my dad was beaming from ear to ear. He'd sold five cars in one day, which was a new record at the dealership he worked at. His energy was always infectious as he told stories about befriending his customers. That night, over my mom's famous Italian spaghetti and meatballs, I learned an invaluable lesson: when you make people feel good, they trust you. And their trust leads to sales.

The Lesson: People Buy from Those They Like

Sales isn't just about closing deals; it's about building relationships. People want to do business with those who make them feel comfortable, heard, and valued. A smile and a good laugh can break down barriers faster than any sales script.

THE POWER OF A SIGNATURE STORY

This one is a little out-there, but my grandfather used to have a game he played with us as kids called "Pinky's Going to Get You."

He'd knock on the bedroom door, whisper that Pinky was entering, and then slowly inch closer until he pounced, tickling us until we cried with laughter. It's something that sticks with me to this day, and I even used to carry this story on with my boys when they were younger.

Years later, I realized that the best salespeople have their own "Pinky" stories—signature moments that stick with customers. These stories make you memorable, relatable, and human.

The Lesson: What's Your 'Pinky' Story?

Find a story that makes people laugh, think, or feel something. Stories sell because they create emotional connections. Whether it's a childhood memory or a funny experience, use storytelling to build relationships that go beyond business.

CONFIDENCE: DON'T LET ANYONE BULLY YOU

One of the most important lessons I learned about confidence came long before I ever set foot in a sales meeting. It happened on the asphalt during a game of schoolyard baseball. A bigger kid tried to take my baseball mitt, which I'd bought with money I earned from my paper route. I wasn't about to let that happen. I fought back and got my mitt back.

That moment changed everything. I stopped hanging around with kids who kept their heads down and started surrounding myself with people who carried themselves with confidence. Years later, in sales, I realized that rejection is just like that bully—it tries to shake your belief in yourself. But confidence isn't arrogance; it's knowing your value, standing firm, and learning from every experience.

The Lesson: Confidence Closes Deals

In sales, if you don't believe in yourself, why should your customers? Walk into every sales call knowing your worth. Stand firm, even when faced with rejection. Every 'no' is just a stepping stone to a 'yes.'

INDIVIDUALITY: WHAT MAKES YOU DIFFERENT?

The unifying theme of the lessons I learned in my youth taught me that life isn't just about numbers; it's about connection. The best salespeople are those who find what makes them unique and use it to their advantage. Whether it's humor, persistence, confidence, or storytelling, lean into what sets you apart.

Find your signature move, and you won't just be another salesperson—you'll be unforgettable.

CHAPTER 9

Time to Get to Work [The 1960s]

LOST AT SEA

At age fourteen, I was on a foggy ocean voyage with my Sea Scouts group. We lost sight of the lighthouse and feared for our lives. A leader told us to pray, and I did my best to steer us clear of any trouble by using my gut instincts. Minutes later, the fog lifted, revealing the lighthouse ahead.

The Lesson: In Moments of Uncertainty, Trust Your Instincts

In sales, there will be times when you don't have all the answers. Trust your training, experience, and gut feelings to guide you through challenging deals.

I was sixteen, and I wasn't just looking for a job—I was looking for a way to take control of my future. My family was struggling. My mom wasn't working, and my dad was sick, struggling with mental illness. Money was tight, and I knew I had to step up.

Determined to land a job, I visited store after store in my neighborhood, submitting applications and speaking with managers. I must have talked to at least a dozen different people, but I kept hearing the same thing: "We're not hiring."

Then, I met Mr. Patino. He was different—seasoned, sharp, a leader. I could tell he knew business, and I wanted to learn from him. We had a great conversation, but when I asked for a job, he told me to check back in a week or two. Most people would have left it at that, but I didn't.

Every week, I showed up. I asked if there were any openings. I made sure he saw my face, knew my name, and felt my enthusiasm. After four weeks of relentless follow-up, he finally looked at me and said: "You really want this job, don't you?"

Then came the words I'll never forget: "You're hired."

That was the first time I truly closed a deal. The thrill of winning that job—of earning it—was unforgettable.

The Lesson: The Fortune is in the Follow-Up

Most salespeople stop after one or two attempts. The great ones? They keep going. Whether you're selling a product, pitching a deal, or trying to land a job, persistence separates the winners from the rest. People don't always say yes the first time, but if you continue showing up, and prove to them you are serious, you'll eventually get your shot.

A SENSE OF HUMOR GOES A LONG WAY

It was my first day working as a box boy at a neighborhood market when the assistant manager asked me to go to the store across the street to borrow a "bag stretcher." I did as I was told, only to be met with laughter at the other store. "Kid, there's no such thing!" the manager said.

That's when I realized it was a joke that my co-worker must've played on every new employee.

A few days later, I found a $20 bill in the store and turned it in. The same assistant manager pocketed it, and to this day, I don't know if he ever gave it to the rightful owner. But I never regretted doing the right thing.

The Lesson: Keep Things Light and Stay Honest

Humor breaks the ice, builds rapport, and makes people remember you. And honesty? That's the foundation of long-term relationships. In sales, make people laugh and always do the right thing—it will set you apart from the rest.

HOW PLAYING SPORTS HELPED BUILD MY SALES CONFIDENCE

I played baseball, football, basketball, and swam competitively as a kid. My peers called me "Big D" because I hit long balls— singles, doubles, and home runs. Being good at sports gave me confidence, which later helped me in sales.

The Lesson: Practice, Practice, Practice

Just like in sports, sharpening your sales skills requires repetition. The more you train, the more confident you become. When you know your pitch inside and out, you can walk into any sales call ready to win.

THE CHOKING INCIDENT—
SLOW DOWN AND STAY IN CONTROL

One afternoon, while working at the market, I nearly choked on a piece of meat while rushing back to work after lunch. I panicked but managed to pull the obstruction out just in time.

The Lesson: Just Like Eating, Selling Should Never Be Rushed

Take your time with each client, build trust, and don't force a sale. Success comes from patience and precision.

A LOVE AFFAIR WITH MY HAIR

In my senior year of high school, I made the first-string football team. I was excited, but there was one problem . . . the coach wanted everyone to shave their heads and get a 'crew cut' before our first game.

Now, I wasn't just any football player. I had *long* hair. I thought of myself as a surfer—okay, maybe a *Hodad* (someone who looks like a surfer but doesn't surf much). Either way, my hair was part of my identity.

Out of over sixty players on the team, I was the only one who refused. Then, one day, six of my teammates surrounded me.

They told me they were going to hold me down and cut my hair. I was outnumbered, but I decided to stand my ground.

I told them, "If you try to cut my hair, I'll fight you all."

I had no idea how it would play out, but something amazing happened . . . they backed off. Fast forward to our senior team photo: I was the only player with long hair.

The Lesson: Stick to Your Guns

Great salespeople don't follow the crowd—they create their own path. The best closer in any company doesn't sell the way *everyone else does*—they find their unique style and master it. Trust yourself. Stick to what works for you. And most importantly, never let anyone pressure you into changing what you believe in. In sales, competition is fierce. There will be moments when you feel up against the wall. When that happens, take a deep breath, block out the noise, and rely on what you've learned. Just as my teammates came to respect me for standing firm, your customers and colleagues will respect you when you stand by your convictions and focus on solving their problems.

GOING THE EXTRA MILE PAYS OFF

At eighteen years old, I was still working at the market but found myself wanting to learn how to use a cash register. A co-worker told me about Charlie, an older checker who would take breaks during the graveyard shift. So, I showed up late at night during one of Charlie's breaks and learned how to use the register on my own time, and wasn't paid for it.

The next day, my manager called me into his office, and I honestly thought I was going to be fired. Instead, he told me, "You're promoted!"

In the days that followed, I became a checker.

The Lesson: Initiative Sets You Apart

No one will hand you success—sometimes you have to take it. If you go beyond what's expected, opportunities will follow.

PLAYING IT SAFE

When I was eighteen, I learned another important lesson that almost cost me my life, but looking back, it also helped shape my sales philosophy. I was taking a joy ride with some friends, which found us recklessly speeding down a winding mountain road. The car lost control, and we ended up skidding dangerously close to a cliff, but miraculously, the car stopped just in time.

The Lesson: Risky Behavior—Like Overpromising or Cutting Corners in Sales—Can Lead to Disaster

Your life and health are your greatest assets. Protect them. And when it comes to selling, avoid being reckless, because your reputation is often your greatest asset.

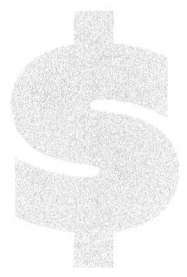

CHAPTER 10

Sowing the Seeds of My Sales Career [The 1970s]

SCHOOL'S OUT, BUT NOW WHAT?

Since I was in the third grade, my mom had always dreamed of me becoming a dentist, and I wanted to make her happy. None of my older siblings had finished college up to this point, so I felt a strong responsibility to make her proud and earn a degree.

Four years after graduating from high school, I earned a BS degree from the University of California, Irvine, and attempted to gain admission to dental school for several years afterwards. But after applying to programs all over the country, I faced rejection time and time again. It took me all those years to realize that dentistry wasn't my calling—it was actually my mother's dream that I become a dentist, not mine. Accepting that truth was painful, but it was also freeing. It forced me to ask myself: *What was I truly meant to do?*

I still wasn't sure, but life moved fast in the meantime. I got married a week after graduation, and within four years, we had two boys. As the sole provider, I returned to work at a Safeway supermarket. I started as an assistant manager, learning the business inside and out, but what I really learned to master was *people*. Every day, I interacted with customers, co-workers, and vendors. I learned how to connect, listen, and influence decisions. Without knowing it at the time, I was laying the foundation for my future in sales.

The Lesson: Rejection is Redirection

Just because a door seemingly closes on you doesn't mean you've failed. Sometimes, it's just life pushing you toward where you truly belong. In sales, you'll hear "no" more times than you can count—but every rejection is just a step closer to the right opportunity. Persistence, adaptation, and self-awareness are key.

DRESS FOR SUCCESS

Shortly after starting my job at Safeway, my manager called me into his office and gave me a warning letter because my shirt was wrinkled. He told me three things:

1. Your job must be a priority.
2. Always dress professionally.
3. First impressions matter.

Since then, I've made sure to dress sharply every day. Years later, this point was reinforced by a sales trainer who told me that "people typically judge someone within the first thirty seconds of meeting them."

So, while dress codes may have relaxed over the years, being neat, stylish, and confident still makes a huge difference.

The Lesson: Appearance Matters

People judge you within seconds, and looking like a professional gives you an edge in the sales world.

STARTING SMALL TAUGHT ME A BIG LESSON

My journey back into the world of sales started somewhat unexpectedly when a co-worker turned me on to a side hustle he'd started doing, which was selling rugs. He said he could get me involved, and that I'd make $3 for each one I sold. I wasn't sure where exactly he was getting these rugs, but I accepted the challenge. With no fancy sales pitch, I simply talked to people, and by the end of that first week, I had sold ten rugs.

That experience opened my eyes. Selling wasn't just about the product—it was about connecting with people. Later, when I got my first corporate sales job, the sales director gave me some advice that stuck: "Talk to at least two new people every day. Whether face-to-face, over the phone, or through email, because making new connections is the key to success."

The Lesson: Always Be Open to New Opportunities

Every experience teaches you something, even if it's not glamorous. Build relationships daily—any conversation could lead to a sale or a long-term partnership.

VISUALIZING SUCCESS—AND MAKING IT HAPPEN

After the birth of my first son in 1973, I put a down payment on my first house. It was a fixer-upper—leaky roof, stained carpet, in terrible shape—but I saw its potential. I envisioned what it could be, and I made it happen.

Years later, I realized that this same mindset applied to my career. Whether it was breaking into sales, closing big deals, or achieving financial success, I always saw the vision of it first. And visualization helped turn my goals into reality.

The Lesson: See It Before You Sell It

Great salespeople don't just pitch a product—they *paint a picture*. They help the customer *see* how their life or business will improve. If you can create a vision that excites your buyer, you're already halfway to closing the deal.

MY FIRST BIG SALES OPPORTUNITY

At the age of twenty-four, I got a call from my dad that he was going to have a major lung surgery after doctors had spotted a tumor, and he wanted to take me to dinner before he went in. I had no idea at the time that this would be the last meal we'd ever share. Over steak and lobster, he told me about the work he'd been doing selling advertising space for the local phone book. He had been doing it for years, and he was good at it—so good that people told him he "could sell ice to an Eskimo."

During dinner, I asked him, "If anything happens to you, who would I talk to about taking over your accounts?"

He told me whom to contact, and less than a week later, he passed away. Shortly after his funeral, the owner of the phone directory called me before I'd even considered reaching out to him.

It seemed that my dad had mentioned me to him, and he wanted to know if I was interested in taking over his accounts. I took the job part-time, while continuing to work at the market, and within five years, I turned a $900 per year commission (which was almost $6,000 per year in today's world) into $42,000 annually (almost $200,000 today)—more than I was making as a full-time manager of a supermarket.

The Lesson: Opportunities Come to Those Who Are Ready

You never know when the right opportunity will present itself, but when it does, you must be ready to act. The best salespeople are always prepared, continually learning, and always seeking opportunities to capitalize on the moment.

DON'T LET DISTRACTIONS DERAIL YOUR SUCCESS

During the 1970s, I dealt with a lot of family challenges—aside from my dad's passing, my sister struggled with mental illness, my brother was diagnosed with brain cancer, and my mom carried the weight of it all. But no matter what was happening, I never let it affect my work. In fact, work became my escape. It was a place where I could focus, excel, and succeed.

While handling my dad's accounts that I had taken over and working on gaining new ones, I realized that sales requires mental toughness. Distractions, doubts, and external pressures will always be there, but top performers find a way to stay focused on their goals.

The Lesson: Stay Focused, Stay Winning

Distractions will test you, but true professionals know how to block out the noise and keep moving forward. If you want to be a top salesperson, you need unwavering focus and the ability to separate personal struggles from professional performance.

HOW I WON THE PRICE IS RIGHT SHOWCASE— AND WHAT IT TAUGHT ME ABOUT SALES

In March 1976, my best friend, Greg, called and said he had an extra ticket to a taping of the TV game show *The Price is Right*. I was off that day, so I agreed to go. Greg gave me a crucial piece of advice before we went to be interviewed by the producers to determine which audience members would be selected to be an actual contestant on the show. He told me, "Wear something colorful, and just be ready to make them laugh."

When the show's producers walked through the crowd, I started chatting them up and got them laughing. Lo and behold, during our taping, I was the first person selected to "Come on down!"

Ultimately, I ended up winning that episode's big finale, the "Showcase Showdown," which scored me a boat, a stereo, and a trip to Hawaii!

The Lesson: Confidence and Preparation Go Hand in Hand

In sales, like in life, those who stand out get noticed. You don't need to be the loudest person in the room, but you do need to make yourself memorable.

LISTENING IS THE GREATEST SALES SKILL

Back when I was fourteen, I asked my wealthy uncle how he made his fortune. He told me, "Buy real estate, especially near the ocean."

Years later, at age twenty-seven, I followed his advice. I bought a triplex, and although it wasn't near the ocean, I kept reinvesting until eventually I owned fourteen properties.

The Lesson: The Best Salespeople are Great Listeners

It's always a great idea to be a good listener both in your personal and professional lives. And in the world of sales, your customers will be telling you exactly what they need—you just have to pay attention.

OVERCOMING FEAR TO FIND MY TRUE CALLING

When I was twenty-nine, I had my first big corporate interview for a sales position with a boiler-making company. I got offered the job but got cold feet. A week before Christmas, I turned it down and decided to stay at Safeway as a manager. At that time, we had two boys, with a third on the way. It took me another three years to start looking again, but when I did, I finally decided to pursue my true passion—working in sales.

The Lesson: Don't Let Fear Hold You Back

Every opportunity you pass up is a chance you might regret later. Sales is about taking the leap and believing in yourself before others believe in you.

But luckily for me, I'd soon be getting more opportunities to make sales my full-time job . . .

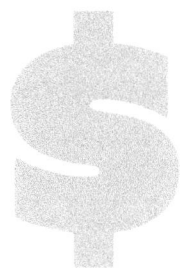

CHAPTER 11

Diving Into the World of Corporate Sales [The 1980s]

A LIFE-CHANGING MOMENT

I was working as the assistant manager at the Safeway supermarket early one Sunday evening in 1981. I was handling a money order transaction near the front of the store, and as soon as the customer I was assisting left, I locked up the money drawer and turned my attention elsewhere—until I felt the cold steel of two guns pressed against my ribs.

Two gunmen had flanked me on either side, demanding that I reopen the drawer and hand over the cash inside. My hands shook so violently that I could barely get the key into the lock. I tried to stay calm and kept reassuring them that I would comply.

After I gave them the money, they turned their attention to the store's safe. Back then, safes had a fifteen-minute timer, but by sheer coincidence—or fate—I had just accessed it to retrieve some money for the store's registers, so it was still unlocked. Inside was $6,000, which was a pretty substantial amount back then.

Then, as I was bent over inside the safe and handing over the cash, I heard a gunshot. Time seemed to freeze. I thought I'd been shot. I turned my head and saw chaos erupting at a nearby cash register. A checker named Elsa—a mother of nine—had been shot in the eye. She would ultimately survive, but as the scene unfolded, it was like something out of a nightmare.

As the gunmen fled, I locked the doors and called the police. When my manager arrived, his first question was, "How much money did they get?"

I couldn't believe it. People were traumatized, a woman lay bleeding on the floor, and he was worried about the money? He then asked a box boy to clean up the blood. This moment was truly a wake-up call.

That night, I went home and drank a bottle of whiskey until I threw up. When I finally woke up the following morning, I decided to leave the grocery business for good. I wanted a career that gave me purpose and control.

The Lesson: Every Crisis Holds an Opportunity

This terrifying experience taught me that life-changing moments often come disguised as adversity. If you feel trapped in a job that doesn't fulfill you, take a step back and ask yourself, "What is my ultimate passion?"

Don't wait for a crisis to push you—act now.

BACK TO SCHOOL

After experiencing the robbery, I couldn't shake the feeling that I needed more. That experience woke me up. I realized I wanted control over my future, and that meant more than just having a steady job—I needed a career that allowed me to grow, challenge myself, and be rewarded for my efforts.

So to sharpen my sales skills, I decided to go back to school at California State University, Los Angeles to get a master's degree in business (MBA). Ultimately, I was a straight-A student in every sales-related course, which helped me prove to myself that I'd found my true calling in life.

The Lesson: Pressure Creates Diamonds

The most challenging moments in life often push you toward your most significant breakthroughs. High-pressure situations in sales—whether it's a tough negotiation, a big deal on the line, or a demanding customer—are what shape you into a top performer. Instead of fearing adversity, embrace it. That's where growth happens.

WAITING FOR THE RIGHT ONE

While pursuing my MBA, I occasionally visited the campus recruiting department and interviewed for sales positions. My first few interviews, which were with companies that sold items like steel and Dictaphones, didn't feel right to me.

But then I met Jimmie, who was a sales manager at a Fortune 500 company (which means they were ranked as one of the top 500 corporations based on their revenue in America), and they focused on selling water treatment, soaps, and chemicals. Within three minutes of us chatting, he told me, "You'd be perfect for this job."

I was confident in my ability to sell anything, thanks to the experiences I'd had thus far, but I didn't jump on the opportunity immediately, as I still had a few months left to complete my degree.

Three months after completing my schooling, I called them back and asked if the position was still available. It was, but they told me there was one condition: I had to meet with the company president first.

The Lesson: Persistence Pays Off

Whether pursuing a sale or a career, you must be willing to keep pushing forward. Sometimes, waiting for the right opportunity and having the patience to see things through makes all the difference.

KNOWING YOUR VALUE

The company flew in its president from Chicago to interview me. After about an hour of tough questions, he made me an offer of $1,400 a month, plus a car and benefits. It was a fair deal—but I knew I could do better.

I had a wife and three kids. I needed to ensure I was making the right financial decision. So, I negotiated. I didn't just accept the first offer that came along. Instead, I asked for what I needed, and I got it.

The Lesson: Know Your Value and Don't Be Afraid to Negotiate

The best salespeople don't just close deals—they ensure the deal works for them, too.

DAY ONE OF MY FIRST BIG CORPORATE JOB

It was 8:30 a.m. when I met my new sales manager at a restaurant. We had a quick coffee before heading out. At 9:00 a.m., we made a cold call to a corrugated box plant in Los Angeles, presenting them with some of the company's hand soap and soap dispensers, which went pretty well.

Midway through our drive, the sales manager received a call and told me he had to go. "Good luck!" he said. "There's a manual—learn one product a week and sell as much as you can."

That was my only training.

By the end of the week, I had sold fifty cases of pink liquid hand soap and five soap dispensers. The secret? I followed his advice. I focused on mastering one product per week, studying its benefits, and selling it wherever I could. It was like being back in school, but it worked.

The Lesson: Knowledge Is Power in Sales

To be a successful salesperson, you must become an expert on what you're selling. Customers trust those who know their products inside and out. Because if you don't believe in your product, how can they?

THE POWER OF HORIZONTAL SELLING

For those unfamiliar with the term, "horizontal selling" refers to offering a product that appeals to a diverse and general audience, unlike "vertical sales," which focuses on a specific industry or niche.

When I started with this company, I didn't know they were the number one hand soap manufacturer in the country. Hand soap is something that appeals to a broad audience, which was perfect for horizontal sales, as it could lead to selling those clients the company's other products.

My first sale was twenty cases of powdered hand soap and ten cases of pink lotion soap bottles. And how did I convince them to buy the products? By taking the customers into their own bathrooms. "Wash your hands," I'd say. "Now feel how soft they are."

That was it—a hands-on demo—literally.

I'd also give hand lotion samples to the receptionists. They'd fall in love with the feel, and pretty soon, I was selling lotion to their whole office building. But here's the key: after I sold them soap, I'd ask what else they used. Degreasers? Disinfectants? Floor cleaners? I'd offer a free trial. Once that door opened, I never left with selling them just one product.

The Lesson: Horizontal Selling Is Where the Real Money Is

Don't sell everything at once. Start small, earn trust, and then build on that trust with every additional product they need. A one-product salesperson has a short shelf life. Start by selling one product, do a great job, then ask what else they use.

MY FIRST BIG FISH

A few months into this first corporate sales job, I landed my first major account because I took the time to research a problem they were facing. It was a carburetor plant that was about to be shut down due to chemical compliance issues. I collaborated with the client and their local regulators to find a solution, ultimately closing a $100,000 deal with them.

The Lesson: Solve Problems, Earn Business

Customers buy solutions, not just products. If you can solve their problems, you will become invaluable to them.

ALWAYS LOOK FOR REPEAT BUSINESS

Selling isn't just about the first order—it's about ensuring continuous revenue. The best salespeople focus on securing second, third, and future orders to establish a stable income stream.

Also, stay on good terms with those you serve, and the rewards will follow. Once, I met an engineer in my early days of corporate selling, who would eventually bring me along as he moved jobs. Over the years, he introduced me to seven new accounts.

The Lesson: Never Just Chase New Customers

Keep existing clients happy so they continue to do business with you. Sales isn't just about persuasion; it's about long-term relationship building. Satisfied customers can bring in business for decades, so treat all of them like lifelong partners.

THE QUESTION YOU SHOULDN'T ASK

In my early days with this water treatment and soap company, I asked a veteran salesperson what time his day started and ended. He just stared at me without answering. I later realized that, in sales, there is no 'clocking in and out'—you are always selling.

The Lesson: Successful Salespeople Are Always on Call

Be available when your clients need you 24/7, and your commitment will pay off.

ALWAYS BE AWARE OF YOUR SURROUNDINGS

During my first year selling for this corporation, I often visited factories in rough parts of town. One afternoon, I pulled over to rest for a few minutes and woke from a nap to a guy tapping a gun against my window. Thankfully, I'd left the car running and sped away before anything could happen.

The Lesson: Always Be Aware of Your Surroundings —Physically and Professionally

Not only should you be safe out in the field, but it also helps to be hyper-aware of your marketplace as well by knowing your competitors, industry trends, and customer needs, so you can always act swiftly and decisively.

ALWAYS RESPECT YOUR CUSTOMER'S BUDGET

I spent a year prospecting a local hospital before eventually closing the deal. Everything went smoothly for the first two years of the contract. However, in the third year, they were required to seek out bids from competitors. Thinking that they had some flexibility, I raised the service price by $100 per month, but to my surprise, I lost the account because my price suddenly exceeded their strict budget constraints.

The Lesson: If a Customer Gives You a Budget, Trust That It's Real

Stay within that budget unless they explicitly indicate flexibility. If they must go out for bids, help guide the process by recommending competitors with higher pricing. Above all, maintain a strong partnership with your customers—be transparent about price increases and provide clear justifications for them. Ultimately, when a customer tells you they have a budget, believe them.

HAVING A VISION AND THINKING BIGGER

In the early 1980s, I was driving over the Angeles Crest Mountains with a technician named Kent, whom I'd recently hired to assist me with servicing accounts. As we descended the winding mountain roads into the Southern California high desert, we noticed the city of Palmdale's rapid growth as an emerging aerospace hub that was buzzing with opportunity.

I turned to Kent and said, "We're going to own this town. Just give it a little time, and let's work as a team."

A few years later, I'd expanded my sales territory by 50 percent and brought in over $200,000 in new sales in that area, which is equivalent to almost three times that amount today. Most salespeople at my company managed to gain only $40,000 in new sales each year, but what set me apart was that I had a vision, which I paired with action.

I didn't just sell products—I also created a new way of selling. I proposed a mobile laboratory that could drive to our customers, offering live demonstrations and customized solutions tailored to their needs. I mapped out a detailed plan, pitched it to the company executives, and got approval. That mobile lab transformed our business and set the stage for my success as one of the company's top salespeople nationwide. Within ten years, I'd built a three-million-dollar sales territory.

The Lesson: Success in Sales Isn't Just About Pushing Products; It's About Innovation

The best salespeople think outside the box and find ways to stand out. Always have a clear vision of where you want to go and align your actions with it.

THE BUBBLE DISASTER

While setting up my first major aerospace account, I made a significant mistake by using a foaming cleaner in a cooling tower, which is an open-air water recirculation system used in large buildings for air conditioning. The result? A giant bubble bath that covered the executives' cars and floated into the air like a scene from a slapstick comedy. I stayed calm, found a solution, and saved the day.

The Lesson: Know Your Products Inside and Out

Selling isn't just about closing deals—it's about delivering on promises. Read product manuals, understand their applications, and never sell something without knowing exactly how it works.

IF YOU'RE STUCK, GET CREATIVE

I spent months trying to win another major aerospace account out in Pico Rivera, only to realize that the purchasing manager simply didn't like me. Instead of giving up, I reassigned the account to a seasoned salesperson who had a better rapport with the decision-maker. As a result, we won the bid and proved our superior capabilities.

The Lesson: If You Hit a Roadblock, Don't Just Keep Pushing—Find Another Way

Whether it's enlisting a colleague, adjusting your strategy, or rethinking your pitch, creativity can help you turn challenges into victories.

THE POWER OF REFERRALS

After building a relationship with the team at one of the aerospace companies in Palmdale, one of them provided me with a lead on another potential client within my territory. With that referral, I landed a new $100,000 account.

The Lesson: Use Referrals to Your Advantage

Once you serve a customer well, don't be afraid to ask them for referrals. Oftentimes, they're more than happy to hook their colleagues and friends up with a trusted recommendation.

BUILD RELATIONSHIPS BEYOND THE FRONT OFFICE

One of the biggest wins of my career came not from the boardroom but from the breakroom. I once visited a file cabinet manufacturer, where, instead of just meeting with the purchasing team during business hours, I showed up during the graveyard shift, from midnight to 8:00 a.m., to meet the cleaning crew and line workers. I brought donuts, sat with them, listened to their frustrations, and gained insight into their operation from the inside out. No one ever paid attention to them, but I did. And they remembered that.

Weeks later, when the company was deciding who they were going to award a large account to, those same workers advocated for me behind closed doors. That connection sealed the deal.

The Lesson: Never Underestimate the Influence of the People Doing the Work

Build authentic relationships with everyone, not just decision-makers. The back-of-house team often has the front-row view of what's really going on, and their support can be the secret weapon to winning (and keeping) major accounts.

GETTING OUT OF A MAJOR JAM

I secured a big deal with a container manufacturer, supplying a chemical that prepped metal drums for a major company that produced jams and jellies. Everything was great—until the coating began to fall off. Instead of panicking, I called in reinforcements, studied the issue, and found that a pH imbalance was the problem. We fixed it, and that account eventually became one of my biggest wins.

The Lesson: Mistakes Happen

The key is to take responsibility, find solutions, and make it right. Customers appreciate persistence and problem-solving more than perfection.

FOLLOW-UP IS CRITICAL

I made a cold call on a large pharmaceutical company and was initially told they were happy with their current vendor. Instead of giving up, I followed up every two weeks, offering more value points each time. On my fifth visit, the facility manager said, "Since I see you more often than my current vendor these days, I'm gonna give you a shot with a three-month trial."

After three months, I secured the account, and they went on to become one of my most loyal customers for decades to come.

The Lesson: Follow-Up Is the Lifeblood of Sales

If you don't stay in touch, someone else will. Make yourself a familiar face, and persistence will win you more business than any pitch ever could. And today's technology makes it easier than ever to keep in contact, since you can use email, texts, and messaging on websites like LinkedIn. Regardless of the methods you choose, it's always good to let them know you haven't gone away.

THE PERKS OF EXCELLING IN CORPORATE SALES

For ten consecutive years, I won an all-expenses-paid trip to Hawaii for being in the top 5 percent of the company's sales force. This included a $750 bonus to spend however I wanted.

The Lesson: You'll Reap the Rewards

Hard work and top performance in sales can bring you bonuses beyond just a paycheck, and consistently excelling can lead to some incredible benefits.

BEAUTY BEATS BRAWN . . . SOMETIMES

After one trip I took to Hawaii with my wife for a week, I returned to find out I'd lost one of my biggest accounts to an attractive blonde woman who had swooped in while I was away. I ended up getting the account back only six weeks later, but it was a reminder that sometimes, you're not going to win just because you're the better salesperson.

Another time, I was told I wasn't "technical enough" for a complicated account. They gave it to someone else. However, I kept part of the business because the decision-maker considered me their friend.

The Lesson: People Buy from Friends, Not Just Experts

You don't have to be the smartest person in the room. Sometimes, you have to be the one they like and trust the most.

BREAK BREAD, BUILD BONDS

A fellow rep once told me: "If you eat at a customer's table, you'll have them for life."

That stuck with me. When you dine with someone, you're no longer just a vendor—you're a person. And people like doing business with other "people," as opposed to someone who's all business, all the time.

The Lesson: Make a Personal Connection with Customers

Lunches, coffees, even five-minute chats in the break room—they all build trust. Get out from behind the desk and make face-to-face contact with clients regularly, which can often lead to forming personal connections with them.

NO ONE SUCCEEDS ALONE—ASK FOR HELP

One of the biggest lessons I've learned in my career is that success is never a solo act.

Back in 1985, I was managing the company's largest sales territory on the West Coast. I worked day and night, putting in the hours, but eventually, I hit a wall and desperately needed help. So, at our annual sales meeting, I made my case. I had all my numbers, all the profits, and I laid it out for my manager, the company director, and the CFO.

Their response? "Figure out how to pay for it."

So, I did. I put together a solid plan, and soon enough, I had the support I so desperately needed—a right-hand person to handle the legwork. It changed everything. Think of it like real estate agents who have assistants—the best in the business don't do it alone.

The Lesson: Don't Be Afraid to Ask for Help

Sometimes, when your sales numbers grow exponentially, so do the demands that come along with servicing your clients. When that happens, don't risk burning yourself out, and don't be afraid to ask for help. Ultimately, you'll need to "sell" your idea to higher-ups, and make them realize that their return on investment will pay off.

THE POWER OF MENTORSHIP

Success in sports, like in sales, isn't just about physical ability; it's about mindset, belief, and the support of a great team. Every top athlete has a mentor, a coach, someone who believes in them and pushes them beyond their limits. That's what I had with my friend and co-worker Doug Teate, one of the best salespeople I've ever met.

Doug and I worked together for nearly sixteen years, sharing sales strategies, brainstorming ideas, and laughing about our experiences. We had each other's backs in sales and in life. One night, we walked into a segregated nightclub in East Chicago, which was in a predominantly Black area, with Doug being Black, and me being the only white person in the place. Without hesitation, he said to me, "I've got your back," and I told him I had his as well.

That was the foundation of our friendship: trust, respect, and shared experiences. I learned a lot from Doug over the years and always valued his expertise and ability to help me solve problems. He always made me want to be a better salesperson and pushed me to become the best.

The Lesson: Find a Mentor, Someone Who Pushes You to Be Better

Sales can be tough, but having someone in your corner who believes in you will keep you going. Just as every athlete needs a coach, every salesperson needs guidance and support.

TIME FREEDOM

Sales is one of the few careers where you can truly control your own schedule. I learned early on that my results mattered more than how I spent my day. My manager once told me, "I don't care what you do during the sales day—even if it's going to bars or clubs—just hit your numbers."

However, that freedom still comes with responsibility. Your schedule must adapt to your customers, and the effort you put in will have a direct impact on your success.

The Lesson: Sales Is a Game of Trust and Self-Motivation

The best salespeople aren't micromanaged; they are self-driven. Build a schedule that works for you, stay disciplined, and earn trust through positive results.

THE POWER OF MULTIPLE INCOME STREAMS

Even when I landed my first corporate sales job, I continued to hold my part-time advertising sales position. I quickly realized that corporate sales gave me the flexibility to manage my time, as long as I hit my quotas, since no one was tracking my every move. That freedom allowed me to build multiple income streams, which ultimately gave me financial security.

Sales is one of the few careers where your earning potential is virtually unlimited, since your paycheck isn't based on hours worked—it's based on results.

The Lesson: Don't Rely on One Paycheck

The best salespeople think like business owners. They create multiple revenue streams and take control of their financial future. If you're in sales, don't settle for just a base salary—find ways to maximize your earnings and build wealth over time.

CONFIDENCE BREEDS SUCCESS

I've read numerous motivational books over the years, and back in the 1980s, I came across an exercise that Dennis Waitley recommended in one of his books. He wrote that before heading into a pressure-filled situation, you should "look at yourself in the mirror, wipe your hand down your face, wipe a smile on it, and state, 'I AM THE BEST!'"

I still practice it every day, on every call I make, no matter how bad a morning or day it has been. This little trick he suggested has helped me many times throughout my sales career.

The Lesson: Make Confidence a Daily Practice

Confidence isn't something you are born with; it's something you build every day. Just like an athlete warms up before a game, a salesperson must prepare their mindset before stepping into a sales call.

FINDING A WAY BACK IN

After losing one of my largest accounts, my manager told me we'd have to wait three years to try to win them back. But I refused to accept that. I analyzed my contacts, strategized, and remembered a conversation with the president of the account I'd lost, who was an Italian man named Guido. He told me, "Call me if you ever need anything."

I took a chance, called him, and within five weeks, I had won the account back.

The Lesson: Persistence Pays Off

Never assume a lost deal is gone forever. Keep relationships alive and utilize every available resource. In sales, knowing the right people can be just as important as knowing the right product.

HOMEWORK NEVER GOES OUT OF STYLE

Years ago, I was invited to speak at a national sales meeting about how I consistently opened new accounts. My answer was simple: I did my homework.

Success in sales, like success in school, requires preparation. I taught my son this lesson when he complained about schoolwork. "The more homework you do," I told him, "The greater your paycheck will be."

He applied that lesson in his own career and became a respected teacher and artist.

The Lesson: Do Your Homework

Research your prospects. Learn about their needs. The more prepared you are, the better positioned you'll be to close the deal.

TAKE GOOD CARE OF YOUR EXISTING ACCOUNTS

During my time with the soap and water treatment company, a market research study revealed why sales were stagnant despite new business efforts: poor customer retention. Many salespeople were so focused on landing new accounts that they were neglecting their existing accounts.

I learned this the hard way when I lost my largest account. I was devastated, but my boss, Dan, had no sympathy. His advice? "The only thing you can do is SELL MORE."

That message stuck with me throughout my career.

The Lesson: Make Nurturing Your Nature

Your existing accounts are your foundation for consistent income and future growth. Strong relationships with existing customers will help you secure repeat business and referrals, ultimately leading to greater success in the long run.

THE WRONG CAR IN SAN FRANCISCO

While travelling to San Francisco on a sales call, I was picking up a rental car and mistakenly drove off in someone else's identical candy-apple red Cadillac. When my co-worker and I were about a mile away from the lot, they noticed a hat and a garage door opener in the back seat that weren't ours. Realizing the mistake, we quickly returned the car, where a very confused and frustrated Chinese gentleman was waiting for its safe return.

The Lesson: Always Pay Attention to Details!

In sales, being observant and alert can prevent stupid mistakes and improve client interactions.

CUT BAIT ON DEAD WEIGHT

While organizing a major golf tournament for key clients, I sought assistance from my sales manager at the company, but he failed to contribute. I then escalated the issue to upper management. The next thing I knew, he was no longer with the company!

The Lesson: Don't Be Afraid to Call People Out

If someone on your team isn't pulling their weight, don't hesitate to speak up. Success in sales is a team effort.

POSITION YOURSELF FOR SUCCESS

After becoming the top salesman at the company, I was invited to spend a week with the senior executives at a luxury hotel in Palm Springs for a company retreat. This was an exclusive group—ten upper managers, all between the ages of forty and sixty. Every day for ten days, we played golf. I always seemed to end up on the winning team because I was consistently paired with the company president. To this day, I'm not exactly sure how the score was kept, but I wasn't about to complain.

The Lesson: Proximity Creates Opportunity

Success in sales doesn't just come from making the numbers—it also comes from how you position yourself. Being invited into the right rooms, spending time with leadership, and aligning yourself with decision-makers can accelerate your career in ways that pure sales performance alone cannot.

The week in Palm Springs wasn't about golf; it was about proximity. By consistently ending up on the company president's team, I was unknowingly building a relationship that mattered. Even though I didn't control the pairings, I understood the importance of showing up, being a good sport, and creating positive interactions in a non-business setting. Those moments translated into deeper trust and credibility back at the office.

In sales—and in any career—your job isn't only to win deals; it's to make sure you're visible in the right circles. Performance opens the door, but relationships keep it open. Position yourself where opportunities can find you.

STEP UP TO NEW CHALLENGES

After our first round of golf on the retreat, one of the company heads turned to me and said, "Since you know the area, why don't you plan the week's evening activities?"

I wasn't prepared to plan the week's itinerary, but just like that, I was given the responsibility of curating top-tier dining and entertainment for some of the company's most powerful individuals.

Luckily, I had spent weekends in Palm Springs before, visiting a friend who was a member of a prestigious golf club. We had dined at some fabulous restaurants, so I felt confident in my ability to deliver. But I wasn't about to rely on memory alone—I grabbed the Yellow Pages (back when that was the go-to resource) and got to work researching.

The Lesson: Be Prepared to Step Out Into the Unknown

In sales, you never know what you'll be asked to do. Step up to challenges outside your comfort zone, and you'll earn even more trust and credibility.

KNOW YOUR AUDIENCE

The first restaurant I picked was a bit of a surprise. The food was great, but some of my colleagues couldn't stop talking about the old waitresses "with blue hair" who worked there. They teased me about it when we got back, and I just shrugged it off. But the next night, and the nights that followed, my choices hit the mark. I made sure to mix it up—high-end dining, live music, and a legendary piano bar where a singer crooned Frank Sinatra and Dean Martin classics. By the end of the week, everyone was raving about the incredible experiences I'd selected for us to share.

The Lesson: The Best Salespeople Understand Their Customers

Pay attention to what people enjoy and tailor your approach to meet their needs. Bringing joy to customers helps build strong relationships and leads to repeat business and referrals.

GIVE PEOPLE WHAT THEY WANT, AND YOU'LL GET WHAT YOU WANT

At the end of that company retreat, my colleagues and superiors praised my choices, and we shared countless laughs. What started as an impromptu responsibility evolved into an opportunity to strengthen my relationships with key decision-makers within the company. I wasn't just the top salesman anymore—I was the go-to guy, the lead dog in the pack.

This experience reinforced a principle, initially provided by sales guru Zig Ziglar, that I've lived by throughout my entire sales career: "If you give other people what they want, you will end up getting what you want."

That week in Palm Springs wasn't just about selling—it was about understanding people, delivering value, and proving my ability to handle more than just sales.

The Lesson: Success in Sales—And in Life—Is About Creating Value for Others

Do that consistently, and you'll always come out

ahead. So, whether you're closing deals, building relationships, or planning the perfect dinner for a room full of executives, remember: the secret to winning is making sure everyone else wins too.

AN UNEXPECTED DISCOVERY

I had an account where we were using a chemical in a waterfall paint booth system to help solid matter (which in this instance was excess paint) rise to the water's surface for easier removal, as long as the water's pH stayed above neutral. On paper, everything checked out. But something wasn't right.

So, I showed up late one night to investigate. That's when I saw it: workers were urinating into the booth. Not out of malice—just convenience. However, it dropped the water's pH below neutral, which ruined the chemical's effectiveness.

Once we addressed the issue (discreetly and professionally), the system worked as intended, and we saved the account. The customer appreciated the fact that I had cared enough to show up and solve the problem at its root.

The Lesson: Never Assume—Observe

The real challenges often live in the margins, at odd hours, or behind closed doors. The best salespeople don't just follow up—they show up. Be present, ask questions, and go where the problems are hiding.

The Evolution of a Salesman
[The 1990s]

THE MAGIC OF SALES

I've always believed sales has a little magic to it. The kind that grabs people's attention, makes them lean in, and leaves them wondering, "How did they do that?"

That feeling started early for me, watching my grandpa perform coin and card tricks when I was a kid. He was a pro golfer by trade, but in his free time, he became a skilled amateur magician. I was mesmerized, but like all great magicians, he never revealed his secrets.

Decades later, I was at one of my son's football games when I noticed a man wearing a jacket that read: "Magic Castle Member." If you're not familiar, the Magic Castle in Hollywood is one of the most exclusive clubs for magicians in the world. I was completely intrigued. I asked him how someone can become a member, and his response floored me: "You've got to study magic, pass a live audition judged by professional magicians, and earn your way in." Challenge accepted.

I spent nearly ten years learning the craft—sleight of hand, misdirection, and stage presence. Finally, I decided to go for it. I performed my act in front of over twenty seasoned magicians, and after a nerve-wracking week of waiting, I got the call: I was in. Since then, I've performed tricks for receptionists, friends, prospects, and even at kids' birthday parties.

The Lesson: Magic and Sales are About Preparation, Presence, and Performance

You're capturing attention, telling a story, and leaving an impression. Plus, it's never too late to learn something new that sets you apart. Whether it's magic, public speaking, or mastering a new industry skill, keep learning. Because just like in magic, the more practiced and polished you are, the more unforgettable your performance becomes.

THE POWER OF PERSISTENCE—OUTSIDE OF WORK

In my early forties, I found myself standing in front of a worn-down, seventy-five-year-old house. It wasn't much to look at, but I saw something different—potential. I had a vision to tear it down and build something new; something that reflected the rising property values in the area. The only problem? I still owed $185,000 on the place, and every bank I talked to said the same thing: "Pay it off first, then come talk to us."

Most people might have walked away. But I've always believed that persistence is a salesperson's greatest asset—whether you're selling a product, a vision, or yourself.

So, I didn't stop. I started where I could. I needed plans. The first architect quoted me $12,000—far out of my reach. But instead of giving up, I asked around. A neighbor mentioned someone who did his plans for $3,000. That connection saved me thousands and helped keep my dream alive.

Nine months later, I had a completed architectural plan, but still no bank loan. I went from bank to bank—nearly ten in total—pitching my vision, trying to convince someone to believe in me. I heard "no" more times than I could count. But then, finally, I got a yes.

The kicker? The bank manager who approved my loan happened to live just a block away from the property. Maybe that made the difference? Maybe it was fate? Either way, I had my shot.

I got the loan, tore down the old house, and started building my dream home.

Eventually, I ran into another snag—no money left for landscaping. I went back to the same bank. They said they couldn't lend me more. But I was honest with them—I told them I'd level the dirt and leave it. No pretense. Just transparency.

The assistant loan manager walked into the bank manager's office—yes, the one who lived on the next block—and came back with good news: they were giving me the extra funds I needed.

All in, I invested about $385,000 into that home. Today, thirty years later, that house is worth over $2 million.

The Lesson: Persistence Isn't Just About Pushing Forward

It's about being resourceful, building relationships, and believing in the long game. Whether you're trying to close a deal, get a foot in the door, or turn an idea into reality, success often goes to the one who keeps showing up when others quit. Even outside of sales, every "no" is just a step closer to the right "yes." Every closed door is a chance to find an open window. In sales, as in life, persistence paired with strategy can be unstoppable. So be relentless. Be creative. Be honest. The results may not come overnight, but with the right mindset, they will come.

SELL SOLUTIONS, NOT JUST PRODUCTS

In one case, my company was offering a product that was a chemical concentrate, where just one gallon could produce fifty-five gallons of usable product. It wasn't just more efficient—it was safer, and easier to store compared to any other product on the market at the time. Previously, the customer was forced to use a product that needed a ratio of 30 percent concentrate that they would need to mix with 70 percent water. Now, with our product, they would need to keep a much smaller inventory of concentrate drums on hand. And the overall cost would be less. That product sold itself.

When I showed them how it could cut their chemical usage in half without sacrificing results, it wasn't even a hard sell. The math made sense, the results were visible, and most importantly, it simplified their operations.

That initial trust paved the way. Once they saw it worked, they continued to come back for other solutions. I didn't just sell them a product; I sold them a solution. I became their trusted advisor.

The Lesson: Don't Just Sell What Your Product Is—Sell What It Does

Help the customer visualize the value: savings, safety, efficiency. When you can prove those benefits and deliver on them, you're not just making a sale—you're opening the door for many more.

TRUSTING IN YOURSELF

Let me tell you about a time when trusting myself not only saved the day but also taught me a powerful lesson about sales. I was on vacation with my two younger sons, Ryan (who was 14 at the time) and Michael (who was 9), exploring the rugged beauty of Northern California's Kern River. Michael, the cautious one, stayed safely on the shore while Ryan and I decided to brave the rapids—a decision I would never forget.

Before I knew it, the current had us. We were being swept downstream, caught in the powerful force of the river. Ryan looked at me, fear in his eyes, and said, "Are we going to die?"

That moment was terrifying, but I knew panic wouldn't help. I grabbed his hand, looked him in the eyes, and said, "Trust me. Hold on tight. We're getting out of this."

We fought through the current, trusted in each other, and made it safely to shore. That experience stuck with me because it proved that belief in yourself is the most powerful tool you have, even in the most challenging situations.

The Lesson: Believe In Your Ability to Navigate the Rough Waters

Sales can feel like being caught in a raging current. There will be tough negotiations, rejection, and moments when you doubt yourself. Trust in your skills, experience, and instincts. When you do, you'll find a way to the shore—closing deals, overcoming objections, and achieving success.

And this was a good lesson to learn at the time, especially since I was about to be blindsided by some unexpected news . . .

FROM THE TOP TO THE BOTTOM IN AN INSTANT

My company had recently hired a new manager, whom I hadn't met yet, and he reached out to me to meet him one morning at a restaurant. He met me in the parking lot and told me that I was being let go. No "Thank you." No exit plan. Just "We're going in a different direction."

After sixteen years as a top salesman at the company, I was unexpectedly laid off. I walked away stunned—but not defeated.

I immediately contacted an attorney and secured a $33,000 severance payment, which would help fuel my quest to become an even better salesperson for the next company that would bring me onto their team.

The Lesson: Resilience Is Key

Rejection and setbacks are inevitable in sales. The difference between a great salesperson and an average one is their ability to bounce back stronger. Keep moving forward.

REBUILDING MY CONFIDENCE

After being laid off, I called a headhunter named Paul, who was eager to receive my résumé. He said, "You've got gold here. Let's polish it up."

Putting my wins on paper reminded me that I was still that guy.

In the weeks that followed my job loss, I interviewed for a new position at another, smaller family-owned chemical and water treatment company. The CEO was skeptical about my salary and asked me to show him my last pay stub. When I did, he matched my salary and hired me on the spot.

Although the company was smaller than my previous one, I was thrilled to accept the job, as it offered a range of new opportunities and challenges that would help me evolve as a salesperson.

The Lesson: Your Experience Is Transferable— Don't Underestimate It

Just because you're in a new place doesn't mean you start from zero. Bring your tools, your contacts, and your confidence, because even though who you're working for might change, your results and relationships go along with you. Also, know your worth! In sales, confidence and evidence of past success can be the key to securing the best base salary.

STARTING OVER—WITH JUST ONE ACCOUNT

After sixteen successful years at a large corporation, starting over wasn't easy. I was the new guy again, and to get me started, they handed me one existing account: a dairy, which was worth $72,000 in sales a year and took up two full days a week just to service.

After a month, I walked into the CEO's office and said: "You're wasting your money. Pay someone else to service this. Let me sell—and I'll make you ten times what this account brings in."

He listened to me, and that move changed everything for the better, both for me and for the company.

The Lesson: Know Where You Add the Most Value

Be honest about where you're worth the most to your company. Don't be afraid to ask for a better use of your time if you can back it up with solid reasoning.

BRINGING BIG EXPERIENCE TO A SMALLER POND

Since I'd taken every class I could find related to water treatment and chemicals while working at my previous job, I came equipped with that knowledge. I also amassed an extensive amount of experience selling to big hitters in the aerospace industry, like Northrop, Lockheed, Rockwell, Vought Aircraft, and many others.

So, when I got to this new company, I already knew more than anyone else in their water treatment group. That confidence, and the contacts I brought along—which were earned through real experience—allowed me to go get some big accounts fast.

During this time, I also decided to further invest in my knowledge, and enrolled in some more chemistry courses at LA Trade Tech. It wasn't required, but it changed the game for me. Furthering my education gave me increased confidence, credibility, and eventually earned me even more commissions.

The Lesson: Don't Wait for Someone to Tell You to Take It Up a Notch

Your expertise is your briefcase—and it never gets outdated. Always keep learning and adding tools and knowledge to your arsenal!

TURNING ONE BIG PHONE CALL
INTO A $300,000 SALE

When I joined this new outfit, my old accounts were off-limits for eighteen months due to a non-compete clause I'd signed. But I still had the contacts. And the trust.

But having to start fresh didn't hold me back. My first big sale at the new job came from a cold call, during which I sold a $300,000 per year aerospace account over the phone, without even meeting the customer. That deal alone boosted my paycheck from $7,500 to $10,000 a month—a 33 percent jump. Then I kept going—calling old contacts, making more cold calls, and slowly rebuilding my book.

The Lesson: Relationships Outlast Restrictions

Even if you can't call on old accounts right away, stay in touch. They remember how you treated them—and that trust doesn't expire.

THE POWER OF STAYING IN TOUCH

My next big win while at this new company was landing one of Northrop's aerospace facilities. From there, I heard they were opening a new branch in another part of town—and my contact was being transferred there. Because I kept in touch, I had the inside track on the new site before anyone else.

The Lesson: Stay Connected

Your next deal might be with someone you already know. Every customer is a seed, so stay in contact even when they move, because often they'll bring you along with them.

CREATIVE PROSPECTING: FROM BINOCULARS TO CHAMBER DIRECTORIES

One of our reps at a company-wide meeting once said: "I used binoculars to look through fences and read chemical drum labels!"

We laughed—but hey, he got the lead.

Me? I used to grab Chamber of Commerce directories from every city in my territory and cold call down the list. You may not be able to sneak peeks through fences anymore, but prospecting never goes out of style, and nowadays there's a lot more information that can be found online, and quickly!

The Lesson: Hustle Beats Hope

Creative prospecting often leads to successful results. Get out there. Research. Knock. Call. Email. Ask.

NEVER LET A TIP SLIP AWAY

A friend tipped me off that the West Coast base of the United States Marine Corps, one of their largest bases in the country, Camp Pendleton, needed help getting their wastewater treatment up to current environmental standards. I didn't know much about municipal systems at the time—but I did know how to learn. With help from our company VP and my own drive, I discovered they had nine treatment plants across eighteen square miles. I began visiting weekly, helping them get back into environmental compliance. After I successfully got them back on track and earned their trust, they began buying everything from me—equipment, chemicals, and many other products.

The Lesson: Follow Tips

Show up. Ask questions. Learn fast. Being a student of your customer's problems makes you indispensable.

BE THE SALESPERSON WHO'S ALWAYS THERE

Camp Pendleton's facility manager once told me, "Dave, I will always use you because you respond immediately."

That stuck with me.

The Lesson: Reliability Wins Long-Term Loyalty

Your availability and responsiveness are often more valuable than your prices or products.

STAY IN TOUCH WITH WINNERS

After I parted ways with my previous company, I still made it a point to stay connected with my best friend in the sales world, Doug. Even while working for different companies, I often called him for help with some of my major accounts. His expertise and insights not only helped me close deals, but he also continued to teach me the importance of fostering relationships with my existing clients and contacts.

Staying in touch with Doug paid dividends at the new company too, as it helped me triple my sales over my first two years with them. I also became a leader within the company and was ultimately given control over an entirely new arm of their business.

The Lesson: Build Strong Relationships and Stay Connected

You never know when an old co-worker might be able to help you grow as a salesperson, both mentally and financially.

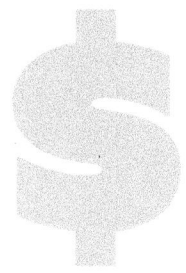

CHAPTER 13

A New Era of Sales [The 2000s]

PILING ON SALES SKILLS TO BUILD WEALTH

Years ago, I started noticing a trend among friends and family: they were buying properties and paying agents 3 to 6 percent commissions. Meanwhile, I was already selling every day in my own industry. It hit me: why pay someone else a commission when I could learn the business and keep it myself?

So, I studied, passed my real estate exam, and started using my license to buy and sell properties. I didn't make a career out of it, but I've consistently sold one or two properties a year for the last twenty-five years—and I've saved tens of thousands in commissions doing so.

Beyond that, I began investing. One day, I borrowed against a property and used it as a down payment on another. I even bought an empty lot, hired the contractor who had remodeled my home, and built a multi-unit rental that now practically pays for itself.

This wasn't a get-rich-quick plan. It was about applying my sales mindset—persistence, value evaluation, and negotiation—to long-term wealth building.

Plus, it's always smart to keep sharpening the tools in your toolkit. Learning skills like real estate or stock trading not only broadens your perspective, but it also gives you options. If you ever decide to pivot out of sales, having another industry in your back pocket means you're not starting from scratch. You're stepping into something new with a running start.

The Lesson: The Best Salespeople Think Like Investors

Whether you're investing time, money, or in relationships, you're building something for the long haul. And just like in sales, the more innovative and more strategic your moves, the greater your return.

WORK SMARTER, NOT HARDER

When I was in my fifties, the president of the company I was working for gave me one piece of advice that changed my career: "Learn to work smart, not hard."

At the time, I had already been selling for decades. But once I started applying this principle, my income started growing exponentially. So, what does "working smart" actually mean?

It means realizing that you can use technology to make life and work easier, that not every prospect is worth your time, and that it's best to focus on the right customers. It also means that you need to identify high-value clients and invest in those relationships.

Time is a commodity that you should never waste foolishly. Leverage your experience. Learn to read people, anticipate objections, and tailor your pitch to each situation.

Finally, utilize your network, as strong relationships can open doors. The best salespeople don't sell—they *connect*.

The Lesson: Anyone Can Hustle, but True Sales Mastery Comes from Strategy

Don't just work harder—work *smarter*. Find ways to maximize your efforts, streamline your process, and build long-term success.

MOVING ON TO GREENER PASTURES

In 2015, after eighteen years of loyalty, hustle, and a whole lot of sweat equity, I found myself at a crossroads. The owner of the family-run company I'd been working for was retiring and handing over the reins to his son. And just like that, everything changed.

I was sixty-five, "retirement age" by most standards, and I wasn't sure what was next. But I knew one thing for sure: my time with that company had come to an end.

So, I gave my two weeks' notice.

Now, don't get me wrong—those eighteen years weren't all bad. In fact, they were some of the most productive of my career. But I had also learned a valuable truth that many salespeople face when working for smaller, family-run businesses: it's not always about merit. Micromanagement, family politics, and decisions made by individuals with little to no field experience can make even the most driven salesperson feel stuck.

I didn't let it stop me. I focused on what I *could* control—my effort, my relationships, and my results.

And the results spoke for themselves. When I started, the company had just forty-seven employees and brought in $72,000 in yearly water treatment sales. By the time I left, we had grown to ninety-seven employees, and annual water treatment sales were sitting at $2.5 million. I managed a team of six and was personally responsible for 80 percent of our water treatment business.

As they say, "A rising tide lifts all ships." My work helped that company grow more than it had in its entire existence.

But when the tide changes, smart sailors know when it's time to chart a new course.

The Lesson: Know When to Walk—and Be Proud of What You Built

Sometimes the best move in your career is the one you *don't* see coming. It takes courage to walk away, especially when you've given years to a company. But great salespeople aren't just driven—they're *self-aware*.

They know when a situation no longer serves their growth. They understand the difference between loyalty and stagnation. And most importantly, they recognize their own value, even when others don't.

If you've built something meaningful, take pride in it. Let your track record do the talking. And when the time comes to move on, do it with your head held high—because greener pastures aren't found by standing still. They're found by moving forward.

TREAT YOURSELF LIKE YOUR BIGGEST ACCOUNT

There I was, at the age of sixty-five and unemployed. I asked myself a critical question: *Do I keep working, or do I retire?* If I were going to keep going, which a big part of me wanted to, there were three things I needed to do:

1. **Improve My Physical Health:** I wasn't in great shape, so I lost forty pounds and committed to working out three to five times per week. Since sales is a high-energy game, if you're sluggish, you'll lose momentum. Staying in shape is paramount.

2. **Sharpen My Mental Stamina:** I found myself getting tired every afternoon, so I adjusted my sleep schedule to get seven to eight hours of rest. Prioritize sleep and recovery. Your mind must be sharp to close deals.

3. **Make Better Lifestyle Choices:** I needed to stay sharp and treat my health like my most important business asset, so watching my diet and alcohol intake became increasingly important.

The Lesson: Always Think Long-Term

Whether you're young or old, you need to be thinking about what lies ahead. Just like in sales, playing the long game leads to sustained success, and your success depends on your ability to perform at your best, both mentally and physically.

GETTING BACK IN THE GAME

I had a good friend who once told me, "If you ever want a job, just call me."

So, one day, sitting in my car in a parking lot, I did just that. He answered, and by the end of the week, he had a pay package ready for me. I got the job working for his new company, which focused on selling fire sprinkler water treatment systems to prevent corrosion in pipes.

Over the next year and a half, I successfully maintained my income by securing significant accounts, including those of Toyota, major food manufacturers, large warehouses, and other commercial structures. But I'll be honest—selling water treatment for fire sprinkler systems wasn't exactly setting the world on fire. Many buildings didn't even need them. It was a tough grind, and I wasn't feeling great about it. Once again, it was time for me to move on.

The Lesson: Don't Be Afraid to Pivot

Sales success isn't just about grit—it's about knowing when to shift. If a product isn't solving a real problem or meeting a strong demand, it's time to reassess. The best salespeople don't get stuck; they adapt.

ONE LAST LEAP OF FAITH

One day, an old coworker called. He asked if I'd be open to talking with the company he was working for—another chemical company. I wasn't sure at first. However, around the same time, a major university that I had a long-standing relationship with called me, and asked if I could supply them with any water treatment chemicals?

And that was it. That was the call that changed everything. I made the sale as a middleman, and from there, I used all my sales and industry knowledge to become an independent contractor.

Then, this new company I was working for asked me if I knew any businesses that were looking to sell?

I remembered a small chemical company whose owner was nearing retirement, so I helped structure a deal where I represented the company being acquired. I negotiated terms, ensured job continuity for their employees, and even secured a commission package for myself. I also earned close to $75,000 on top of my commissions during the first few years of the acquisition, and I still represent the acquired company to this day.

The Lesson: Your Network Is Your Net Worth

Staying in touch with past customers, colleagues, and business contacts can lead to unexpected, high-value opportunities. Sales isn't just about closing deals today—it's about planting seeds that grow over time.

MUCH MORE TO COME

Ultimately, after joining forces with this independent chemical manufacturer, I helped them acquire two chemical companies with which I'd previously worked.

I still currently represent this company, but we worked out a program where I get all my chemicals from them, which I resell, and use their service team to service some of my accounts. They do all my billing, and I share a percentage of the profits that are derived from my commissions. From the outside, it may look like I work for them, but I run my own company and business through them.

With my commissions, I can pay my help when needed and pay my monthly office rental. I could have started a business from scratch, but I felt it would work out better having a big company behind me. And they turned out to be the perfect fit.

They don't micromanage me. They let me run my own book of business. That kind of trust and autonomy? It brings out the best in people like me. I went from scraping by at the fire sprinkler company to tripling my income.

And that's what I'm still doing to this day, at age seventy-five. With my current role as an independent contractor, I didn't just find a job—I found a company that let me run my business like an owner. No micromanaging. Full freedom. And the results? Now, I'm selling with freedom, confidence, and joy. It's been a fun ride, and it's far from over.

The Lesson: Do What Works for You

Take the initiative to be your own boss. Find out how you work best and do what works best for you, because no one knows you like you!

CHAPTER 14

Looking Back and
Other Lessons Learned

So here I am, at age seventy-five, and selling is still fun! Every day, I'm making a great living doing what I love to do.

When I first started in the chemical sales world, they gave me a briefcase to carry samples. But eventually, I realized my best briefcase was the one I held in my head. I had the knowledge, the experience, and the confidence to speak the customer's language. That's my true sales toolkit—and it's made all the difference.

Although products change, and industries shift, knowledge never goes out of style. Know your stuff. Be the person who can simplify the complex. That's when clients start to *trust* you, not just tolerate you.

Over the years, I've learned that it's all about relationships, and to not ever burn any bridges because it'll come back to haunt you.

I've also had the honor and privilege of working with many other excellent salespeople over the years, many of whom have shared some fantastic stories of their own personal experiences that left a lasting impact on me.

Below you'll find some additional lessons, from my sales stories and theirs . . .

KNOW WHEN TO SHUT UP

One of my favorite teachable moment stories comes from a colleague who was training a brand-new sales rep fresh out of college. They had a meeting scheduled with a corporate purchasing agent in a skyscraper that practically screamed "Fortune 500."

The rookie was nervous—understandably—and launched into a nonstop sales pitch the second they sat down. He didn't ask a single question. Meanwhile, the purchasing agent was distracted, barely made eye contact, and quickly wrapped-up the meeting.

Embarrassed but hopeful, the two headed to the restroom across the hall to regroup. The rookie disappeared into a stall, and, thinking they were alone, started telling my colleague how awkward and rude the purchasing agent had been.

You already know what's coming.

The purchasing agent had walked in quietly and was standing right there, listening. When the rookie chimed in from the stall with some not-so-kind words, the agent let out a laugh and walked out, leaving both men mortified.

The Lesson: Always Be Aware of Your Surroundings—And Your Audience

Sales is about people, and people are everywhere, especially when you least expect them to be. Speak with professionalism, even in private, because you never know who's listening or who holds the keys to the next deal.

THE 80/20 RULE IS REAL

After analyzing over forty years of sales commission sheets, I was able to confirm a statistic that a couple of people had mentioned to me in the past, and that was that "80 percent of your sales will always come from 20 percent of your customers."

The Lesson: Love Your Core Customers

Nurture your big clients. Treat them like royalty. Keep them happy, and they'll fund your future. That small group pays your mortgage, year after year.

TWO NEW PEOPLE A DAY—NO EXCUSES

An old-school sales manager once told me: "Talk to two new people every day."

It's simple, but it works. If you're not out there shaking hands (or calling, emailing, marketing, direct messaging, etc.), then you're invisible.

The Lesson: Don't Just Be Great, Be Prolific

Two new contacts each business day should equal approximately forty each month, and if you stretch that over a year, that should result in 480 new contacts annually. It adds up. Fast.

THE PARKING SPOT INCIDENT

A friend of mine was mentoring a sales rep who struggled with time management. One day, they were late for a critical appointment with a plant manager. The parking lot was packed—except for one open, clearly marked *reserved* spot right up front.

Against their better judgment, the rep parked there, and they hustled inside. It turns out that the plant manager was also running late. Lucky break? Not quite.

Minutes later, shouting erupted from down the hall. The plant manager was furious someone had taken his reserved space, and was demanding to know who it was. My friend and his rep made a quiet exit to move the car before things got worse. But the damage was already done. First impressions matter, and this one screamed, "I don't respect your space."

The Lesson: Punctuality and Preparation Signal Respect

Being early gives you breathing room. Planning ahead prevents embarrassment. And even small details— like a parking space—can have a significant impact on how you're perceived.

THE POWER OF THE BUSINESS CARD

I've passed out thousands of business cards over the years. One of our employees at my current company told me she found my cards all over the place—at restaurants, at customer sites, even in random office drawers.

That's the point. You never know who might pick it up. And here's the trick: I always made my cards funny or memorable. Something that stood out. One time, when I became the number one salesperson at a Fortune 500 company in the 1980s and 1990s, I was offered a regional manager job, but I turned it down, as I'd make less money.

Instead, I asked them to create a custom title: Key Account Specialist. It meant I could sell anything, and that title *stuck*. It also looked intriguing on my cards and helped break the ice with new clients on many occasions.

The Lesson: Business Cards Still Work

Make your business cards unforgettable. Cards are cheap, and so are digital ones. Make them unique. Make them sticky. And hand them out like candy. You're planting seeds.

Also, when you happen to grab cards or contact info from anyone, always hang onto their personal phone number. At the very least, store it in your phone, and always stay in touch. Even many years later, they'll remember you if you've helped them in the past, even if they've moved onto another company.

DECISION-MAKERS CAN BE ANYWHERE

Sales opportunities are everywhere—you just have to be open to them.

A colleague of mine was waiting in line for a beer before an Ohio State vs. Michigan football game, decked out in Ohio State Buckeye red. Behind him stood a Michigan fan, and naturally, a little good-natured trash talk ensued.

Then came the casual, "So what do you do for a living?"

It turns out the Michigan fan was a key decision-maker at a facility my friend had been trying to gain access to for years. Right there in line, he gave a thirty-second pitch. By Monday, he had a meeting on the books.

It led to product trials and eventually, a new account.

The Lesson: Always Be Ready with Your "Elevator Pitch"

Whether you're at a boardroom table or in a beer line, know how to sell yourself and your product clearly and confidently. You never know who you'll run into over the course of any given day, so it's always best to be prepared.

MAKE YOURSELF UNFORGETTABLE

Most of my customers call me "Double D," and I've had that nickname on my business card for thirty-five years. I learned the value of a nickname from a college instructor. It's a simple trick—but it sticks.

The Lesson: Branding Isn't Just for Companies

It's for people, too. Stand out. Be memorable. A good nickname beats a forgettable title every time.

ALWAYS KEEP YOUR PIPELINE FULL

The business of selling is all about momentum. You can't just sit back after one big win. You've got to keep calling, keep prospecting, and keep closing so when one deal ends, another begins. Otherwise, you'll be scrambling to meet quotas later down the line.

This is how I built a territory from scratch and grew it into $3 million in annual sales with nearly $1 million in profit. Not by luck. Not by shortcuts. By consistency, creativity, and connection.

The Lesson: ALWAYS Be Selling

Work today for a deal that closes in six months. Your future you will thank you.

PREPARATION BEATS PERSONALITY

One of my buddies from the sales world was a classic Type A personality—fast-talking, confident, always ready with an answer. He built a strong relationship with a key contact at a company, who told him he'd be happy to set up meeting for him to pitch the company's decision-makers. He also told my friend that he shouldn't worry too much about preparing for the pitch, since he felt it was going to be an automatic "slam dunk." So naturally, he didn't prepare.

The presentation went smoothly—until the Q&A portion came. That's when someone lobbed a tough question he hadn't even considered. Instead of admitting he didn't know, he talked in circles, trying to sound confident. "Great question! The answer is really threefold . . . "

But it wasn't. He babbled. The room went cold. The sale was lost.

The Lesson: Confidence Is Great—But Preparation Closes Deals

If you don't know the answer, it's okay to say so. It shows honesty, humility, and professionalism. Sales isn't about knowing everything—it's about knowing how to get the answer.

GET PERSONAL: LUNCHES, SANDWICHES, AND HOLIDAY PARTIES

I've always believed that "people buy from people," and people eat. Therefore, I used to bring sandwiches to one of my top accounts every couple weeks. Even if they couldn't leave for lunch, they'd sit down for five minutes over a sandwich. We'd talk. I'd listen. And the relationship would grow.

I also donated raffle prizes for customers' holiday parties every year. It built goodwill, and they remembered me when it mattered.

The Lesson: Relationships Close Deals

Food, gifts, and genuine conversation go further than you can imagine. Be human first, and a salesperson second.

THE 'TOP TEN TARGET' RULE

One gem I picked up from a sales seminar was to keep a list of your top ten prospects, and touch base with each one every two weeks. If they fall off the list, then make sure to stay in touch at least once a year.

The Lesson: Out of Sight Is Out of Mind

Keeping your name in front of key accounts isn't about spamming them with meaningless check-ins or cluttering their inbox. It's about being intentional. Every interaction should reinforce your credibility and remind them why choosing you was the right decision. That might mean sending an article relevant to their business, dropping by with a quick update, or offering a fresh perspective on an industry challenge they're facing.

NEVER OVERPROMISE JUST TO WIN FAVOR

Years ago, a sales manager I knew hired a former Heisman Trophy runner-up. The guy had name recognition, charisma, and could walk into just about any office and get a meeting. But that was the problem—he relied *only* on his reputation.

At one point, he promised a VP he'd show up at his kid's football fundraiser. The VP was thrilled and hinted it could lead to some real business between them. But the rep never showed. He didn't even call to say he couldn't make it.

His manager spent months doing damage control, but the relationship—and the opportunity—were both dead.

The Lesson: Under Promise, Over Deliver

In sales, trust is currency. Never make a promise you can't keep just to win favor. Show respect for your customer's time, expectations, and values—and your reputation will carry more weight than any trophy ever could.

CHAPTER 15

Finding The Elusive Work / Life Balance

THE BALANCING ACT WE ALL FACE

If you're in sales, you already know it's more than a job—it's a lifestyle. The thrill of the chase, the buzz of closing, and the constant drive to be the best. But here's the truth: if you're not careful, that lifestyle can take over your *entire* life.

If you're anything like I was—a full-blown workaholic—then you already know the truth: family and work are always sitting on opposite ends of a seesaw. And most days, it feels like you're the one in the middle trying to keep both sides from crashing to the ground.

Can we ever truly find a perfect fifty-fifty balance? Honestly, I'm not sure. Some days, your career needs everything you've got. Other days, your family does. What I *do* know is this: the balance isn't a destination—it's a daily decision.

For years, I felt like a juggler, tossing priorities in the air, trying to keep them from hitting the floor. That constant act of juggling—of being present at work without disappearing from home—is what I now call "avoiding the salesperson trap."

The trap is simple: You pour everything into your clients, your sales numbers, your next big close . . . and before you know it, the people who matter most are getting your leftovers.

After spending over four decades in sales, I've learned—often the hard way—how crucial it is to find balance. Over that time, I've gathered some insights that are worth sharing, in the hopes they might help you achieve balance in your own life.

1. BALANCE STARTS IN THE MIRROR

Balance starts with awareness—the ability to recognize when it's time to give your all to the job, and when it's time to be fully present at the dinner table with your family. However, true balance extends beyond simply choosing between work and home.

At the center of it all is you. If you're not taking care of yourself—physically, mentally, and emotionally—then neither side gets the best version of you. You are the hinge that holds both ends of the seesaw, and if you break, everything around you wobbles. Balance isn't just about time management; it's about self-management.

It means not treating sleep like an optional luxury, but as the fuel that helps you make smart decisions and stay emotionally grounded. Yes, that's right—sleep is one of the most underrated sales tools out there. You can't lead, sell, or build anything meaningful if you're running on fumes.

In the high-stakes world of sales, mental health isn't a luxury—it's a necessity. This industry is filled with pressure: performance targets, rejection, long hours, and the constant drive to outdo yesterday's success.

It's easy to fall into the trap of believing you have to be "always on," always grinding. But the truth is, your mind is your most valuable asset—and if you don't take care of it, everything else suffers.

Sales requires resilience, confidence, emotional intelligence, and clarity. You can't lead with empathy, handle objections, or build meaningful relationships if you're running on stress, burnout, or anxiety. Prioritizing mental health—through rest, boundaries, support, and self-awareness—isn't just good for you. It makes you a *better* salesperson, a better teammate, and a better human being.

2. FAMILY FIRST—THEY'RE YOUR FOUNDATION

I'll be honest: there were stretches in my life when I spent more time with customers than my own family. Sound familiar? Ask yourself: *Am I giving my best to the people at home, or just what's left over after work?*

Here's what worked for me:

- I make sure we eat at least one meal a day together. It's not about the food—it's about the connection.
- We do small projects together—landscaping, painting, whatever. The point isn't the task, it's the teamwork.
- If you're married or have a partner, I suggest scheduling a date night once a week. Not when it's convenient. Not when the stars align. Put it on the calendar—just like you would with your top prospect. This simple habit kept my connection alive through all the long hours and travel. Sales can consume you. Don't let it consume your relationships.

- I encourage my partner to have hobbies, too. We both need our own space to grow individually.

And me? I enjoy meditating in the mountains or by the beach whenever I can. Even a walk in the park or sitting down with a book does the trick. Balance doesn't have to be expensive—it just has to be intentional.

3. STAY PRESENT WITH YOUR KIDS

Sales often demands your time, energy, and attention. But your children deserve that, too.

- Make sure to show up at their games or other activities they participate in.
- Help them with their homework (even if it's math you've long forgotten).
- Spend time with them *one-on-one*, not just in group settings.

What's the point of working twelve to fourteen hours a day if you miss the chance to build real memories with the little people who think you're a hero?

4. BALANCE ISN'T ABOUT WORKING LESS—IT'S ABOUT WORKING SMARTER

As mentioned earlier, a good friend once told me before he retired, "Work smart, not hard."

I didn't get it at first. It took me years—and a lot of missed moments—to fully understand.

5. DRAW THE LINE BETWEEN WORK AND HOME

Yes, sometimes you have to bring work home. But make it the exception, not the rule.

Closing big deals gives us a high—it's addictive. A therapist once told me: "If you're a top-tier salesperson, you might be borderline manic."

She wasn't wrong. Sales can feel like a drug. But if you let it control you, it will.

6. LEARN TO SAY "NO"

This might be the hardest lesson of all, especially when you *love* what you do.

There were years in my first marriage when I used work as an escape. I told myself entertaining clients at night was part of the job. Sometimes, it was. But other times, I was avoiding the more challenging job of being present at home. That imbalance cost me.

Now, I've learned to say "no" when it matters. You can too. It's not about being selfish—it's about being smart.

7. WHAT I KNOW FOR SURE

- You will make mistakes. We all do.
- You may lose balance at times. That's okay—*just don't stay there.*
- The best friends you'll ever have are at home. Your customers may love you, but they won't sit beside you when you're sick, old, or alone.
- It's something that will always require work. I'm still working on it every single day.

Ultimately, if you want to be successful in life AND sales, you've got to invest in your life *outside* of sales.

FINAL TAKEAWAY

So, here's the lesson I've learned after years on the seesaw: Don't chase a perfect balance, chase *presence*. Be fully in the moment when you're with your clients, and fully in the moment when you're with your family. Don't let the job become your identity. It's what you *do*, not who you *are*.

Sales success means nothing if it comes at the expense of everything else. The best salespeople aren't just great closers—they're also wise enough to protect what matters most: their time, their energy, and their relationships.

Balance doesn't happen by accident. It takes intentional choices, hard conversations, and sometimes saying "no" when everything inside you wants to say "yes."

Ultimately, make those you love your biggest clients. Whether they're your family, your partner, or whoever else you might be closest to, make sure to give them your precious time. Be fully present and follow up with them often. Because in the end, the greatest deal you'll ever close is a life well lived.

AFTERWORD

THE LEGACY OF A SALESPERSON

Looking back on my journey, I see a pattern: my greatest sales lessons came from life's most unexpected moments. Also, selling isn't just about transactions; it's about resilience, preparation, and knowing when to take a leap of faith.

My hope is that these stories inspire you to take control of your career, learn from challenges, and embrace the mindset of a successful salesperson. Because if I could do it, so can you.

As I bring this book to a close, I want to leave you with a few thoughts that have shaped my journey, not just in sales, but in life.

This past weekend, I visited the cemetery in Glendale, California, where five of my family members were laid to rest. As I walked past the gravestones, I stopped by the final resting place of my great-aunt Mary, who lies next to baseball legend, former New York Yankees manager, Casey Stengel. A woman stood nearby, snapping a photo of his tombstone. She was a Yankees fan who was visiting the cemetery as part of a tour.

We chatted for a few moments, and during our conversation she told me how Casey Stengel had won seven World Series championships, and since she was here visiting from Connecticut, she just had to pay her respects.

As she went on her way, I glanced at one of his quotes that appeared on a plaque beside his grave, which read: *"There comes a time in every man's life, and I've had plenty of them."*

That simple statement hit me hard. Life, in all its twists and turns, is just that—a series of moments in time. Brief periods that come and go. The big ones, the small ones, the ones that define you.

I've had my share of sales moments—times of triumph, of struggles, of learning, of closing the deals that seemed impossible. And when I look back, I realize that it's not just about the wins; it's about the journey, the passion, and the people you meet along the way.

I wasn't born a great salesperson, but when I found my true calling in sales, I ran with it.

Now, over four decades later, I'm still at it. And what's more, I'm earning nearly three times what I did in my earlier years. Why? Because I never stopped learning. I never stopped applying the lessons that worked for me.

As I mentioned towards the beginning of this book, one of the first motivational books I ever read was *The Greatest Salesman in the World* by Og Mandino. In it, he suggests that "We are not here that long, so you better be happy with what you are doing."

So, if you're not passionate about your career, change it. The average lifespan is short, so why waste time doing something you don't love? If sales is your calling, embrace it. If it's not, find what lights your fire and pursue it with everything you've got.

I wrote this book not just to share my stories, but to help you create your own. Every technique, every lesson, every piece of advice in these pages has been tested in the real world. If you apply them, if you take action, if you commit yourself to being great, there's no limit to what you can achieve.

Sales isn't just a career. It's a craft. A mindset. A way of life. So go out there. Build relationships. Close the deals. Write your own success story. And most importantly—enjoy the ride, because in the end, "The Greatest Salesperson" is inside YOU.

And now, I'll leave you with a summary of the typical traits I've found in every successful salesperson I've ever met during the course of my career . . .

WHAT CHARACTER TRAITS MAKE A GREAT SALESPERSON?

1. Trustworthiness

2. Being a great storyteller

3. Having a sense of humor

4. Realizing that selling isn't all about you, but it's about the customer and their needs

5. The willingness to go the extra mile for your customer

6. Being able to balance your life between work and family

7. Knowing when to take a break from working to enjoy life

8. Being thankful every day for the business and friendships you've found in the sales world

9. Being able to stay in touch with those people who are responsible for your sales success

10. Being spiritual, and answering to a higher source

11. Giving back to others in the sales profession and sharing knowledge with them . . . *which is the main reason I've written this book.*

BOOKS THAT HAVE INSPIRED ME

Since I've read almost every book ever written about business and sales, I wanted to suggest the ones that had the biggest impact on me. I highly recommend everyone who works in sales to read them as well, if you haven't already:

1. *How To Win Friends and Influence People* by Dale Carnegie
2. *The Greatest Salesman in the World* by Og Mandino
3. *The Little Red Book of Selling* by Jeffrey Gitomer
4. *Seeds of Greatness: The 10 Best-Kept Secrets of Total Success* by Dennis Waitley
5. *Zig Ziglar's Secrets of Closing the Sale* by Zig Ziglar
6. *See You at the Top* by Zig Ziglar
7. *The Power of Habit* by Charles Duhigg
8. *The Seven Habits of Highly Effective People* by Stephen Covey
9. *Think and Grow Rich* by Napoleon Hill
10. *Rich Dad, Poor Dad* by Robert T. Kiyosaki
11. *The B2B Sales Blueprint: A Hands-On Guide to Generating More Leads, Closing More Deals, and Working Less* by Dan Englander
12. *The Millionaire Mind* by Thomas J. Stanley Ph.D.
13. *Secrets of the Millionaire Mind* by T. Harv Eker

ACKNOWLEDGMENTS

First and foremost, I'm deeply grateful to everyone I've worked for—and with—throughout my career. Each of you played a part in shaping the experiences and lessons shared in this book.

A special thank you to Jim Glidden, who handed me a product manual on my very first day in corporate sales back in 1982. During my first year with the company, I'd become one of the top sellers out of nearly one hundred salespeople. Why? I read the manual. I learned it inside and out—and it changed the course of my career.

A big thank you as well to Frank Lutz, the sales director at my first corporate gig, who taught me that how you dress matters as much as how you pitch. And to Al Butler, who didn't just hire me, but believed in me. He and Frank gave me the chance to prove myself and paid me more than any other entry-level salesperson earned at the time. Within thirty seconds of meeting me, they said I was perfect for the job. And I was. That opportunity changed everything.

To my son, Vince D'Orazi, thank you for your help with editing this story. Your sharp eye and honest feedback were invaluable. And to my sons, Michael, Ryan, and Daniel—thank you for encouraging me to share my journey. Your support means more than you know.

To my father, Tony D'Orazi, thank you for letting me watch and learn during your own super-selling years. And to my mother, who always asked me after every big win, "What's next?"—thank you for keeping me moving forward.

I'm also grateful to some of the early readers of this book, including Dan Peterson, one of my longtime sales managers, who shared memorable stories and insights that added real depth.

And to Greg Quon, my friend and financial advisor, who provided me with thoughtful feedback.

I'm also thankful to the Steve Harrison group and their incredible production team, whose guidance helped me pull this lifetime of stories together into a book.

Finally, to my wife, Beckie, thank you for giving me the space and quiet time to reflect, and the time to turn these stories from memories into words. Your honest feedback helped shape this book, and your steady presence gave me the confidence to finish it. Most of all, thank you for walking beside me—not just through the writing of these pages, but through every chapter of our continuing journey.

ABOUT THE AUTHOR

David F. D'Orazi is a career salesman with over four decades of proven success in some of the toughest industries in America. From his first paper route as a kid to closing multi-million-dollar deals, he's lived and breathed the sales life. David didn't just study the craft—he lived the grind, kept the journals, and made the calls when no one else would.

Sales runs in his blood. His father was a born showman turned salesman who could charm just about anyone—skills he passed on to David early and often. Those early lessons—how to connect, how to listen, how to earn trust—became the foundation of a career that would span decades, break records, and shape a philosophy that still holds up today.

After writing the remarkable true stories of his larger-than-life father and Hollywood starlet sister, David now turns the spotlight on himself in *SELL, SELL, SELL!*—his most personal and practical book yet. This time, he's not just telling a story, he's handing you the keys. Packed with real-world lessons, unfiltered insights, and battle-tested strategies, David reveals what it really takes to build a lasting, successful career in sales—year after year, deal after deal.

With equal parts grit, humor, and heart, he's excited to finally share his playbook to help the next generation of sellers find their voice, close their deals, and enjoy the ride.

David holds a biology degree from UC Irvine and an MBA from Cal State Los Angeles, but he'll be the first to tell you that most of what matters, he learned in the field. He still lives in Los Angeles, where he continues to sell, tell stories, enjoy his family, root for the Dodgers, and write books that he hopes will help people succeed—not just in sales, but in their everyday lives. Since after all, even those who don't work in sales still have to sell their ideas to others on a daily basis.

www.ingramcontent.com/pod-product-compliance
Lightning Source LLC
Chambersburg PA
CBHW051318120626
46547CB00015B/2298